I0820342

Block Island

BLOCK ISLAND

Poems, Photos, and Letters

Daniel Berrigan

Edited by Susan Hagedorn and Carla Berrigan

BROWN BOOKS
PUBLISHING GROUP

Block Island
Poems, Photos, and Letters

Brown Books Publishing Group
Dallas, TX / New York, NY
www.BrownBooks.com
(972) 381-0009

A New Era in Publishing®

Publisher's Cataloging-In-Publication Data

Names: Berrigan, Daniel, author
Title: Block Island : poems, photos, and letters / Daniel Berrigan.
Description: Dallas, Texas : Brown Books Publishing Group, [2025] | Includes bibliographical references.
Identifiers: ISBN: 978-1-61254-718-3 | LCCN: 2024951091
Subjects: LCSH: Block Island (R.I. : Island)--Poetry. | Home--Poetry. | Islands--Rhode Island--Poetry. | Nature--Poetry. | Friendship--Poetry. | Social problems--Poetry. | Spirituality--Poetry. | BISAC: POETRY / Subjects & Themes / Places.
Classification: LCC: PS3503.E734 B56 2025 | DDC: 811/.6--dc23

ISBN 978-1-61254-718-3
LCCN 2024951091

Printed in Canada
10 9 8 7 6 5 4 3 2 1

For more information or to contact the author, please go to www.DanielBerrigan.org.

Dedicated to the ongoing peace legacy of Daniel Berrigan

1921–2016

Contents

Note to the Reader
by Susan Hagedorn

This second edition of Dan's *Block Island* tells us the story of a saint in ordinary life, living on an extraordinary island that we shared with him. It tells us the story of the cottage down the road, and the stories told by Dan, of Dan, again and again. It tells us of the gossip of the island; the tiny house on the cliff in the fog; the laughter, the drinking, the appreciations and worries of getting home to Block Island when the boats and planes were canceled; the exaltation of Block Island in the snow; the priest who shared his home with friends, relatives, AIDS patients, other priests, those in need, and my friend Carla.

In 2018, I finished *Seeking Shelter*, a film that accompanied a traveling exhibit and was about Dan, his partner in theological crime Bill Stringfellow, and Block Island's peace legacy. Then, with Hope Reeves, Rick Dresser, and the Reale brothers, we finished another film, *The Berrigans: Devout and Dangerous*, which celebrated the Berrigan family's peace and resistance legacy.

I swam in Dan Berrigan's world for the last decade. I am the unbelievably lucky recipient of Berrigan generosity, mythology, and family. My house dangles off the same cliff as Dan's cottage, sharing the horizon and drenched by the same spindrift, spirit, fog, birds, and wind. Originally, I knew Dan's fabled story of being sought and captured by the FBI on Block Island, but little else.

I'd had very little connection to the Berrigans during the '60s; in fact, I represented the other side of the peace movement, the violent side, in the Weather Underground. While I respected the Berrigans, I would never see myself as nonviolent. Faith-based nonviolent resistance? Not me! But I loved the passion and adventures that folks on Block Island talked about: Dan Berrigan's arrest on the island, Bill Stringfellow's evangelical island leadership, silent peace vigils in front of the turn-of-the-century cinema downtown every week from noon until one, the one cantankerous island resident who regularly harassed the faithful, and dinners for ten with Dan's wildflower stews.

The last decade of my life has been dedicated to the Berrigans' legacy, digging deep into the ways they changed history over a century of resistance. Who would have thought that Sparky, as I was known for the revolutionary fires I allegedly lit in the '60s, would become an acolyte of America's prophet of nonviolence?

Inspired, and living the stories told, down the road from Dan, I read and reread Dan's 1985 collection of interlinked story poems, *Block Island*. The poems we have reprinted are about the relationships, the weather, the isolation, the ceremonies, the gossip, the difficulties that is life on this small town off the coast of Rhode Island, a decade or two behind the times. I recognized the sea, the fog, the people in town, the tragedies and love affairs that were part of our history. Like Thornton Wilder's *Our Town*, Dan Berrigan, in his gloriously sensuous language, shares his life, his humor, and his delirious faith, all made ordinary by being on Block Island. *Block Island* remains Dan's most accessible collection of poems.

With the help of Carla Berrigan, the DePaul Berrigan Archive, Bill Wylie-Kellermann, Jim Reale, the Island Free Library, Father John Dear, and Karen Paul, we've added poems otherwise not published or included in the first edition of *Block Island*, photos of Dan and his cottage on-island, and many, many letters written to family and friends on and about Block Island.

While an internationally beloved (and despised) prophet, priest, and poet in his off-island life, Dan was an ordinary neighbor in this small town, unable to find a plumber and in trouble with his contractor. Dan shared his cottage with friends, those recently released from prison, those ill with HIV/AIDS.

Determined to share this extraordinary out-of-print book of lyrical stories plus other material that further enriches our understanding of Dan, Carla and I joyously bring you *Block Island: Poems, Photos, and Letters.*

> "Start small and stay small and do immediate
> good work. Just do it and be there."
> —Interview with Dan, *Devout and Dangerous*, 2021.

Prologue
by Bill Wylie-Kellermann

It may be that Dan's cottage on Block Island was first hatched as an idea at table with Bill Stringfellow and Anthony Towne when he was underground some days at their place before being captured by the FBI "birdwatchers" in August of 1970. In federal prison for burning draft files as a liturgical protest against the U.S. war in Vietnam, he thought often of Block Island as "a dreamy hammock hung between two worlds . . ." (page 14). In time, within a few years of his release, the house was raised across the meadow on the bluff at "land's end."

Among the important additions to this volume of poetry, so deftly and beautifully amplified from the original, is a poem (find it as a photo on page 114) which Dan had lettered high on the west wall in his distinctive calligraphic hand. (If you peeked inside the closet by the bedroom door you could see where he'd practiced with various markers before setting out.) Some guests still recite it by heart, seeing and reading its imprint burned in memory. I've often thought of it as an exorcism prayer because it invokes a series of protections upon "all who dwell here." Since the cottage was truly a place of hospitality, the dwellers in all were many.

The first version included beneath it a list of (mostly male) resisters who'd enjoyed hospitality there, though folks like the Breyderts, Island nurse Mary Donnelly, or other guests named in these poems may have been included. I was not, though I confess to coveting that membership. Dan references the list in the first poem of this collection:

> Then came friends for healing respite
> out of the city's iron clutch
> the desperate amenities
> of Burial Brigade.
> The names kept on the wall
> like a votive wall
> or a litany of linked loves.
> You know them as do I
> by heart: scholars, cooks, poets
> meditators, for whom sea & land
> are one blessing, like the paste
> of spit and dirt, an unguent
> in the Healer's hand.

Dan's brother and co-conspirator, Philip, was among that list, though he only visited the Island once. It was a traumatic trip. Taking a swim down the bluff, he was swept out to sea by the riptide, leaving Elizabeth and two-year-old Frida on the rocky shore, terrified and powerless. He surfaced far out, swam parallel, and returned safe to terra firma. Mayhap the prayer's hand of protection was upon him, though he never returned to the Island. It was only after his death that Liz herself chanced the journey again. Nevertheless, he was most present here to his brother. In a poem written for Phil in prison, "Your Second Sight," Dan puts on, like glasses, his younger brother's second sight to recognize a clockface washed ashore: "the last hour of the world / the murdered clock of Hiroshima." (Another new addition to this volume. See page 108.)

The wall poem's second iteration, reinscribed after insulation and new wallboard went up, omitted the names but added in their place a small cross and a toothed wolf head in silhouette. The two comported. They represented in different ways the threats of the powers named in the poem—the law's clawed reach, the second death, envy's tooth, and doom's great knell.

The wolf stood in for the predatory forces, but with resonance dearly personal. Dan begins his own autobiography, *To Dwell in Peace*, alluding to the story of Francis taming the wolf that terrorized a town, but uses it to recount, as a child, his face being thrust by an older brother into the snarling open mouth of a wolf corpse hanging in their Minnesota shed. That experience is reprised herein (page 85). A terror gone deep. The cottage, like the Island, kept its vocation for him as well: a safe house, quieting the soul.

As a seminarian in New York fifty years ago, Daniel placed in my hands *The Wisdom of the Desert*, edited with an introduction by Thomas Merton. The essay recounts how the hermits hightailed it for the wilderness when church and empire hooked up. Though heavy weather could blow in, Dan wasn't making so much for wilderness as initiating a practice—regularly stepping off mainland "America" for these environs contemplative and hermitical.[1]

For him, Manhattan and Block Island were "thesis" and "antithesis," and you can feel the city fall away in poems perhaps even jotted on the train en route, leaving behind the "junk heap" of "tin can culture" and "the hellish transport's rebellious roar" (pages 51, 57). In another, riding that very subway's roar, he looks in faces, summons compassion, and like an intercession wishes them the solitude and gifts of the Island and its house (page 16).

It could indeed be said that Dan was in essence joining a monastic enterprise, if one not highly formalized, for that is how Stringfellow described life together on the Island with Anthony Towne. Cloistered by the Island, they sought contemplation vocationally "in the midst of the world."

Truth be told, Bill and Anthony first came to the Island in a threesome. Though he ended up not staying, the first to arrive was Ray Karras, who'd been in the Army with Tony and more recently a teacher on the mainland. He never really took to Island life. Before locating and acquiring "the main house" atop an Island high point, the three had envisioned buying

---

1. See "Contemplative: An Urban Hermit's Place on the Bluff" in Bill Wylie-Kellermann's *Celebrant's Flame: Daniel Berrigan in Memory and Reflection* (Cascade Books, 2021).

land and building. Architectural plans were drawn up for three separate living units connected by passageways to a central common space. But then Ray departed; the hilltop house was found, the designs shelved. Later, when preparations began for the Berrigan cottage, the plans suddenly re-presented themselves. Island contractor Lew Gaffett was simply handed the ready-made blueprints for one of the living units. It was more practicality than conscious design, but Berrigan would reside in one of the original "monastic cells."

Dan had been given freedom, walked the land, and chose the spot. Near the cliff, but not too near. The sea was slowly coming for the house. The view was sumptuous and often restful, but real estate was falling into the sea. In fact, Dan's choice of location was not shrewd in the realtor's sense because a pond behind the cottage's back wall was draining just underground into the Atlantic, hastening the collapse of that portion of the bluff. Muttered the sea: "I'll inch toward it / I'll have the cliff for first course" (page 3).

On the other hand, that trickle was perpetually carving a new path, steep and sometimes harrowing, to be sure, down to the shoreline. Dan would follow a trail, mown in later years, around the rock wall and dense brush, for his descent to the rocky shoals. He'd return, maybe hauling up a flotsam find, often a lobster-pot buoy broken free on the tide, now to be hung in a row of similar prizes from the railing of the cottage deck.

Just a few words of physical description seem in order. A sliding glass door provided the view (toward "Portugal, our nearest neighbor on east," as Anthony would say). An expandable dining room table just inside could be made wide for dinner guests. Dan's culinary skills were notorious. In my experience, at the city table his menu ran toward pasta, but on the Island, fish—baked, broiled, or occasionally grilled—with pasta to the side. The interior was finished by Herb Fisher, Island anarchist and craftsman. He lived very simply and was an inveterate comber of the Island dump, before it was mechanized. Stringfellow told that Herb would attend gatherings in people's homes, survey the contents, and joke, "Someday this will all be mine." Which is to explain that desk and cupboards were fashioned of barnwood with handles made from organ stops reading BASSO PROFUNDO and the like.

The tiny bedroom was itself something of a sanctuary. Like his Jesuit apartment on Ninety-Eighth Street, the walls were full of photos and art, fitted together close. A congregation of beloveds. Something parallel prevailed in the bathroom, though in this case the hangings were plaques of awards. This was not organizational put-down. More like keeping applause in its place, a certain self-mockery or a discipline of modesty.

The love letters *from* this house were also *to* it. Read herein. It was for Daniel a stirrer of dreams, bursting even with resurrection. Teetering on the brink, shaken like a dynamo, our little house unsteady became a metaphor for hope itself. It did not fly flimsy to bits, but even so was mindful of those which had, at one ground zero or another. It was itself a kind of intercession, uttering a night prayer—a spread wing over a fledgling. Faithful, non-betrayer, the house resisted being either shrine or tomb and was definitively NOT FOR SALE. Like the basket of a great balloon, he rode it up, up into the Presence.

The house, and the Presence it bore him into, was his place of reading and, above all, writing. Consider these poems, these letters, first and foremost. Although there was a solid desk just inside, when weather allowed, the deck was Dan's place of choice to write, the Olivetti[2] on a small table overlooking the sea. That salt air breathes in so many of his books. An earth flag (depicting the celebrated view from the moon) was raised at the corner over a hammock. "A porch facing the sea / September noon, late summer haze receding. / Like a dazed microbe, over a microscope / I'm ferreting out Greek scripture, / word for word. Wonderful!" (page 92). Or again (page 80):

> The luxury, this plank porch
> like a raft bobbing in the shallows
> this million dollar
> prospect: me
> king of the raft, grandly setting down lines
> like life lines to the dead.

2. A classic portable typewriter.

I myself had a special relationship to the plank porch. Dan made the place readily available to friends. A calendar in New York kept the schedule. He would drop a note to warn if the summer was filling quickly. His brother, Jerry, and Carol Berrigan were always honored with August. But it was a special offering to those recovering from imprisonment or illness, or contemplating actions. Jeanie Wylie (now of blessed memory) and I honeymooned there in 1984. On firm principle, guests came for free. In fact, there was a little word of welcome, framed and on a bookcase, which outlined arrangements (see page 98). No money was to be exchanged over the place. The digs, like the view, were a gift. If you saw some bit of work that needed doing, feel free, but enjoy. My personal bit of work, annually attended, was to care for the deck. That usually involved a trip to the lumberyard for a few long boards, a gallon of water repellant, and a large crowbar loaned to me each year by Gordon Smith. Sometimes one board led to another and back to the yard.

One year, while I stayed a longer stretch there on my own, I painted the outside—gray-blue stain on cedar shakes. It was serious brushwork, but a delight in the sun and sea breeze; or like the monks say, *Ora et labora.* Pray and work. Toward the end of that time Dan arrived and I moved up to the main house, but Bill and I were invited down for dinner that night. After, as drinks continued, Dan produced a check which he passed before me to Bill. The amount, substantial by my lights, seemed either to be what the paint job was deemed worth or simply some amount of Stringfellow's need. He also pulled from a bookcase and presented to me a clay sculpture of Gandhi's head after a caricature by David Levine. I had to look twice. There was no exchange of money, no quid pro quo; it was a sweet and simple circle, entirely of gifts.

In reply to a letter from me, apparently recounting a cottage dream I no longer recall, a "pome occurred," not otherwise published, part of which read:

> the cottage, arms outspread
> like a mother, like Stringfellow's ghost—Come one, come all!
> Around, scripture or waters ebb and flow—
> no one pays for,
> not a farthing.

No fee, no false fealties, no
low life pennant lording over, only

the sky, fastened to centerpole
anchored to first day,
proclaims original blessing; Be.

Across the lawn out front, Block Island meadow voles scamper along the rock wall setting up house in a crevice. Along the bluff edge a hawk skims close, riding the updraft on a wimpled wing. Wild roses flourish thick between the wall and the cliff. In season, Dan harvests rose hips for tea, more like a tonic to my taste. And something similar with crab apples as well, a compote concoction. Trees are planted in contemplation of memory. The hardiest survivor, a twisted red pine devoted to Paul Mayer's mother, Bertel. Others stay low to the ground or perish in the assault of winter storms.

One stunning new addition to this volume, "DAYS ON AN ISLAND IN JANUARY WILL DO THIS TO YOU," views the yard covered in snow "like a pall on a dead face / Slowly drawn" (see page 101). I read the poem as being about Island time where clocks slow, like people. (Elsewhere he navigates Island culture, noticing the understated gesture of drivers greeting one another with nothing more than a finger lifted.)

But here mid-winter . . .

Waves a league long arrive from Portugal
And die like near-heroes ashore
Spectacular!
They resemble the pharaoh's chariots, horses, and men tumbling
down
Scriptures, expendables, watery warriors

The pharaoh seems to be in his pursuit, ordering him back "where you belong," but we surmise he is free to disobey, or if he goes in cuffs, a smiling resister. The verse was once posted on an Island bulletin board prompting responses and entering lively conversation.

The lives of Islanders are told and named herein, often in recounting their deaths. A series of poems concern Katherine Breydert, survivor of the Nazi regime and liturgical artist whose stunning mosaics and stained-glass offerings grace St. Andrews Church. Even frail and death-bedded, she is elegant, mindful, self-possessed (page 26). There is told an excruciating Island search for two children entombed in an abandoned refrigerator. A silence here. More comic is the escape by death of notorious Island taxi driver, Norma Nordberg of Corn Neck Farm (page 76). And there is likewise a comic touch to the otherwise solemn memorial of Anthony Towne, Stringfellow's beloved partner, replete with an ancient rite of exorcism in a downpour (page 11). Another new addition here, "My last death was William Stringfellow's . . ." (page 106) is really a proclamation of resurrection, with Bill "chasing death pitilessly / dismaying, dispelling death," then ascending straight up.

It's actually remarkable how many poems here are about the dead and their dying. The house was a "campfire toward which the dead crept to warm hands." Grief is a form of love, and this volume is riddled with the one taking the form of the other.

More than once a verse devolves to simply utter a list of his losses. "Who dies, and I do not?" (page 28). Some names are otherwise unaccounted here, some repeatedly and in detail. Young mystic Catholic Worker, John Leary, who crossed over suddenly while jogging in Cambridge, Massachusetts, with a smile on his face, confounding the officers who found him. Or Ken Feit, Jesuit turned vocational fool, entertaining children on the ferry, buried by his family in a tux—or as Stringfellow quipped, "yet / another clown suit" (page 41).

Dan himself officiated at some of these funerals. The burial of Stringfellow's ashes, side by side with Anthony's disinterred from their place by the flagpole of the main house (now long sold) took place a year after the 1985 funeral at which Berrigan had preached. A group of Island folk, plus friends from across the country, received Dan's hospitality that day. He cooked a feast, but first presided for the simplest of rites, though the Book of Common Prayer necessarily had a voice as well. Jim Wallis and I dug the grave. For a marker, a sculpture of Daniel's hands in cuffs flashing the peace sign rested on the adjacent rock wall. In the cottage, a plaque of Dan's design was hung: "Near this cottage the remains of William Stringfellow and Anthony Towne await the resurrection, Amen Alleluia" (page 125).

Or as he put it herein, they were perhaps among those . . .

noble friends, twice ennobled by death
they sup, depart—
transfigured, undefiled,
down cliffside, turn in farewell.
We saw or thought we saw
them
walking sea waves
away, away, into dawn.

(This essay was originally titled "An Island, a House, and a Communion")

Introduction
by John Dear

Daniel Berrigan was one of the most charismatic, brilliant, poetic peacemakers in modern history and my friend and fellow Jesuit for over thirty years. For the last fifty years of his life, Block Island was his secret refuge of peace. As his literary executor, I am thrilled that my friends Carla Berrigan and Sue Hagedorn have brought back this book of poetry, which has been long out of print. It is a celebration of life, peace, and creation itself, which is to say, the God of life, peace, and creation.

Dan's Block Island was much different than today's. It is still a teardrop-shaped island off the coast of New England, but up through the 1970s, it was mainly fields, woods, stone walls, secret trails, inaccessible beaches, and spectacular cliffs, with nary a tourist or a soul in sight. It was the island of the islander, known mainly to those who lived there in season and out. There were few, if any, bikes or buggies or ice cream stores or rental cottages. There was the old hotel, a restaurant or two, the post office, a church or two, and, of course, the ferry.

The ferry ride is the key to understanding the whole Block Island experience. Boarding the ferry from Galilee, Rhode Island, meant leaving "America" and heading off to another country, to the new world. The short trip was always refreshing, renewing, and restoring, as if the breeze and air were fresher and more alive. There was something about being out on that open sea and slowly approaching the beloved island. Almost immediately, all one's worries, anxieties, and plans fell away. One began to slow down, breathe deep, come back to life, and transform into an islander.

When legendary theologian William Stringfellow retired to Block Island from Harlem in the mid-1960s for health reasons, Block Island was rustic countryside surrounded by the ocean. Stringfellow invited his friend, the famous poet, priest, writer, and peace activist, Reverend Daniel Berrigan, to visit him, and thus began Dan's annual visits to the island. Several times a year, he made the trek from Manhattan to the island, where he stayed in a little work shed on Stringfellow's land looking out over the ocean.

Eventually Stringfellow built Dan his own little cottage on the edge of his property, a few feet from the stone wall, a hedge and the cliff leading down to the beach and the ocean. The cottage had one small main room with a handmade desk, old wood stove fireplace, bookshelves, kitchen, bathroom, and bedroom and was surrounded by a deck and a green lawn.

Dan was teaching high school students at Brooklyn Prep in 1957. While there, he published his first book of poetry, *Time Without Number*, which won the prestigious Lamont Poetry Award and catapulted him overnight into the literary world. He would go on to publish at least ten more volumes of poetry. In 1998, I edited his collected poems *And the Risen Bread*, which readers might also like, as well as *Daniel Berrigan: Essential Writings*, which feature his best poems and peace essays.

Dan had long ago surrendered his life to the God of peace. But as the 1960s dawned, now in his forties, he had begun to learn some hard Gospel truths, especially from his friend and mentor Dorothy Day. He saw her serve the poor, day in and day out, but, even more, condemn every war that came along, even refuse to go underground during the New York City air raid drills and be hauled off to jail each year until they were stopped. During his sabbatical year in France, he made trips to South Africa, Czechoslovakia, and Russia, meeting resistance leaders everywhere. Upon his return home, he heard Dr. Martin Luther King Jr. preach in Selma, Alabama, and joined the march. As the U.S. began to bomb North Vietnam, he realized that the spiritual search for the God of peace and the call of Gospel peacemaking demanded a public response, especially from a priest, even though, apparently, no U.S. priest had ever publicly condemned war before—except his friend the Trappist monk Thomas Merton.

And so, the celebrated poet started to speak out vehemently, albeit lyrically, against the war. His steady stream of poetry, journals, essays, and theology books took a sharp turn as he condemned the ever-worsening conditions in Vietnam. In 1965, his Jesuit superiors had enough and ordered him on the next plane out of New York. In an effort to silence him, he was sent to Latin America with no return ticket. They could not tolerate such "politics." Priests, Jesuits, and bishops do not speak against one's nation's wars, he was told. Up until now, their job was to bless the wars, the troops, and the war-makers. Dan broke that imperial spell for good.

Latin America only sharpened his resolve. He returned a year later and accepted a post as a chaplain at Cornell University. Then, in October of 1967, he marched with his students upon the Pentagon in the first mass act of nonviolent civil disobedience against war in U.S. history. Dan spent two weeks locked up, becoming the first U.S. priest ever arrested for social protest. In January 1968, Dan and Howard Zinn were asked to go to North Vietnam to bring back three U.S. POWs who were being released to the U.S. peace movement. When they arrived in Hanoi, the U.S. began its heaviest bombing raids to date, forcing them to hide out underground in a bunker for eight days. It seemed as if the U.S. was directly targeting Dan.

Like Martin Luther King Jr., Thomas Merton, and Dorothy Day, Dan stood up publicly and spoke out boldly against war and nuclear weapons from then on, in season and out, and paid a heavy price for this radical discipleship to the nonviolent Jesus and the Gospel of peace. After Dr. King was assassinated that April, Dan was visited at Cornell by his brother Phil, who invited him to join a daring new nonviolent raid on a draft board outside Baltimore, Maryland. They stayed up all night discussing it. As Gandhi had argued decades before, Phil said they needed to take the initiative, that the U.S. government would allow them to write letters, sign statements, and lead vigils forever, while it continued to bomb, kill, and wage war. They needed to take the lead and attempt some bold drama to wake up the nation.

And so, on May 19, Dan, Phil, and seven others entered the draft board in Catonsville, Maryland, took some three hundred paper draft files, dumped them in the parking lot outside, covered them with homemade napalm, set them on fire, said the Lord's Prayer, and calmly waited for the police. The media had been notified, and *CBS Evening News* filmed it, but Walter Cronkite thought it was too provocative, so it was never shown. Decades later, it appeared on YouTube, where the black-and-white footage is still available for all to witness.

Phil had written a standard statement filled with statistics explaining the reason for their action, but Dan suggested they needed something with more flare. So, he wrote those memorable lines: "Our apologies, good friends . . . for the burning of paper instead of children. . . . We could not, so help us God, do otherwise." Their act made headlines around the world and shocked churchgoers everywhere. Two priests hauled away for protesting the war! That October, they were found guilty in their Baltimore trial, and Dan was expected to turn himself in to Danbury prison after his appeal ran out.

It is hard, fifty years later, to appreciate the shock, outrage, notoriety, and calumny that Dan and Phil incited for their symbolic action. Priests had never challenged U.S. nationalism, militarism, and idolatry. The Berrigans were hated by most churchgoers and mainstream Americans but admired by students and young people who took to the streets in historic numbers. Indeed, there would eventually be over three hundred draft board raids in the next few years, effectively ending the U.S. military's recruitment of young men in the Northeast. To this day, few realize how these symbolic actions literally brought the war to a halt.

Nixon had promised peace but only increased the U.S. bombings, killings, and destruction of Southeast Asia. And so, the Berrigans asked: Why turn ourselves in? So began one of the most famous fugitive stories in U.S. history. After speaking to ten thousand people at an antiwar rally at Cornell, Dan slipped into one of the costumes from a theater troop, hopped on the back of a motorcycle, and sped off into the night with the FBI hot on his heels. With that, his life underground began.

Each week, he appeared in some church or community gathering to speak out against the war and received widespread, positive media coverage. For months, he was featured almost daily on the front page of the *New York Times*. J. Edgar Hoover, the director of the FBI who had wiretapped Dr. King, was livid and ordered a massive FBI search, but they could never catch him. Dan hoped to carry on this innovative antiwar life for years but, after five months, decided he needed a rest. So, he boarded the ferry to spend a few weeks with William Stringfellow.

This is where the drama of Daniel Berrigan comes to Block Island, forever changing his legend and the island's.

The FBI secretly monitored Phil's correspondence in prison and learned of Dan's location. Hoover ordered a massive raid to catch their man. A nor'easter hit the island just as scores of agents raided the house. They ran in from behind the bushes, handcuffed the unarmed priest, and hauled him off. But the FBI agents were not used to the ferry. They all became terribly seasick and threw up violently on the ferry ride back—everyone but Dan. The UPI photographer on the mainland captured a famous photo of Friar Dan in handcuffs with a beaming smile, while the FBI agents on either side of him frowned and looked sick to their stomachs, which they were. It ran on front pages around the world.

Dan spent years in Danbury and was released early in 1972 because of his declining health. He went on to write some fifty books of poetry, journals, essays, and scripture studies, taught in many colleges and universities, and was repeatedly arrested, over two hundred times, for civil disobedience against war preparations. In his nineties, Dan retired to the Jesuit infirmary at Fordham in the Bronx, where he died peacefully on April 30, 2016.

In light of this drama, when the whole world first learned of Block Island and its notorious, peacemaking, fugitive priest, the poems herein take on a new aura: a deeper grace, yet a more urgent tone. They were written over the course of many years visiting the island, as Dan began to slowly heal from prison and notoriety. To my mind, while they each stand beautifully on their own, the whole book is actually one long poem, a true work of art.

Jesuits were not allowed to have their own houses or cottages, so it was unusual that Dan's Jesuit provincials allowed him to stay there. But they were glad that he had a place to retreat and gather his strength. Everyone knew how hard he worked. He seemed to travel the country every week for decades, speaking to every church and college that invited him.

Dan didn't own the cottage. When Stringfellow died, it was left in the hands of friends who set up a trust to oversee it and manage it, as long as Dan was alive. He went there for two-week stretches, two or three times a year. He also lent it to many relatives, friends, other activists, and a long list of people suffering from cancer and AIDS, many who died shortly after their visit to the island and its magical cottage. His little house of peace brought tranquility and freedom to hundreds of friends seeking a respite from America.

I was a young Jesuit, writer, and peace activist when I first met Dan in the early 1980s. He was awaiting sentencing for a Plowshares disarmament action in September 1980, when he, Phil, and others hammered on unarmed nuclear nose cones at the GE plant near Philadelphia to call the nation to begin the process of nuclear disarmament. He was facing up to ten years in prison. He told me about the cottage on Block Island and gave me one of the first copies of the original *Block Island* the day it arrived. Then in the mid-1980s, he invited me to spend a week at the cottage.

I remember the letter he sent with all the details and the hand-drawn map of the island with arrows directing me on a two-mile walk from the ferry to the cottage. Walk to the bench, near the Baptist church. Head up along the coast to the PROPANE sign and turn left. Follow the dirt road and take a second right at the tree. Cross the lawn of the old Stringfellow home, go through the hedges near the pond, and there, standing on the edge of the world, you will find the little cottage. It was like a treasure map that led to our own El Dorado, aptly named "Eschaton" by Stringfellow, the Greek New Testament word for "the end of time and the beginning of the reign of God."

It was the first time I had ever stayed alone in a little cottage anywhere, and the beginning of a new understanding of the spiritual depths of peace. I had spent the previous summer in El Salvador, where I served in a refugee camp out in the countryside. Death squads roamed about, and U.S. aircraft dropped bombs hourly on the nearby Guazapa volcano hoping to kill FMLN (Farabundo Martí National Liberation Front) rebels. I was supervised by the university Jesuits, who were later assassinated in 1989. That summer, I was volunteering in Washington, D.C., at the national office of Witness for Peace, opposing Reagan's war on Nicaragua. So, I was ready for the peace I discovered and the God of peace I met in that humble abode above the cliff.

I would return to the cottage several times a year for the next twenty years until Dan's death. By the early 1990s, I drove Dan there regularly from New York City, and I would stay in the attic of the Catholic parish center. I became close friends with the pastor, Friar Ray Kehew. Every January, when he left the island for his annual break, I would move in and substitute for him in the parish for a month. In later years, I'd bring our Jesuit friends Bob Keck and Steve Kelly, rent another cottage, and we would spend two weeks on rest and retreat, with daily Mass and evening meals together. As I walked its streets, trails, and beaches and got to know the islanders, Block Island became my respite, my retreat, my geography of peace.

Everyone who seeks to live in peace, who seeks the God of peace, needs such a retreat in God's creation where they can walk and breathe and listen to the wind and the waves. It can be the local park or the nearby woods, a river or pond, another beach or mountain or desert, but Mother Earth offers each one of us the geography of peace if we take the time to look and see.

As I savor each line of these poems, I feel again the grace and peace that the Block Island cottage brought Dan and so many of us. Dan went there tired, broken, sometimes sad, sometimes depressed, sometimes angry, but from the moment he settled down on the upper deck of the ferry, facing into the wind, looking out across the sound, he came alive. His issues, struggles, anger, and conflicts fell away. He would find himself renewed, resuscitated, even resurrected. I would, too, and all of us who stayed at the cottage.

According to Anthony Towne, starting in the late 1960s, Dan would spend nearly every day by himself down below the cliff, along the shore, reading and writing poetry. He would only emerge in the late afternoon for cocktails, dinner, and lengthy conversation, usually about theology, politics, cooking, or movies, not necessarily in that order. That became his island rhythm.

I think Dan was inspired to this solitude and peaceful rhythm of prayer, poetry, reading, and writing by Thomas Merton, who moved into his own cottage in the woods on the edge of the Gethsemani monastery in Kentucky. Dan would visit Merton once or twice a year throughout the '60s and stay up late talking with Merton in his hermitage. There, Dan learned the art of contemplation, the love of silence, the quiet joy of solitude, and a childlike appreciation of nature as a necessary balance to his public activism against the war. He knew, too, that Dorothy Day kept a little cottage on the beach on Staten Island, up until her death. Our friend Thich Nhat Hanh also had a cottage retreat where he let go and breathed deep in peace.

For decades to come, this became Dan's routine. He stayed quiet and alone during the day, meditating, writing poetry, reading, and walking the beach. At night, he would host a few island friends for one of his gourmet dinners. He would return to our Upper West Side Jesuit community in Manhattan, ready to take on the culture, to face the next audience or jail cell. The island had healed him, or the cottage on the island, or better yet, the God of the island.

Reading these Block Island poems now, I find new clues about the life of peace and the balance between taking a stand against the culture of violence, war, poverty, greed, racism, nuclear weapons, and environmental destruction and maintaining a quiet inner core of peace, rooted in contemplation, prayer, mindfulness, reflection, forgiveness, compassion, and the wonder of friends, community, and creation. I think the cottage and the island liberated him into peace, and the poems are the fruit of his inner freedom and nonviolence.

Here, Dan writes about the house as a place of peace, prayer, and healing; about the sea and the One who walks the sea; about friends such as Bill Stringfellow, Katherine Breydert, and Bill Kellermann; and about death, an ever-present theme in his work: the death of Anthony Towne (Stringfellow's partner), John Leary (a young Harvard graduate who joined the Boston Catholic Worker and peace movement and then died suddenly while jogging), Ken Feit (a charismatic young Jesuit priest who died in a car crash), and the two boys who disappeared for days on the island only to be found dead inside an abandoned refrigerator. They had been out playing and accidentally, tragically, got locked in and died. The whole island grieved their passing, including Dan.

Is this the house "where doubt is exorcised," the house of "no betrayal," "the el dorado / of holy fools, who / land failing underfoot / walk water?" he asks. This house, he writes, did not blow apart at Hiroshima. "All, all is noon-drenched sweetness / courtesy, reward of sense."

"A good house is one / you send love letters from; / itself good news . . ." he writes. "Go from here, venturesome," he tells himself, "not knowing where." So he goes from there—risen like Lazarus in "blazing resurrection" to undertake "felonious deeds!"

"Here I resolved," the poem confesses: "Be next to / nothing! Shortly / a galling wound healed." On the one hand, he's learning the fine spiritual art of letting go of one's ego and achievements and, at the same time, learning to dwell in "the Presence," or at least the peaceful emptiness of the God of the island. As he let go and let God, so to speak, he was healed from the wounds of family, church, the Jesuits, and the never-ending war. It's a process, a journey, a pilgrimage of peace we all have to undertake.

"Now and again," he writes, "heard in uttermost silence / [the] voice of a summoning bird / tipping the world to innocence. / Gospel moments." In silence, the Spirit of the God of peace spoke to him, and the Gospel of love and peace came alive all over again. That's why he concludes, "Be not astonished" if the house levitates, sings alleluias, and ascends "into the Presence."

Unlike everyone else's house or apartment, this cottage was a doorway into grace, peace, and "the Presence," into God. It was there where he grieved, rejoiced, and was made whole, that he saw "this God I never see / until I forget to look / walking the waves, beckoning." The message he heard from Jesus? "Repent; be made / sane!" You are no longer victim of the insanity of the culture of war and violence, its prisons and racism, its grinding greed and nuclear weapons and mass destruction of Mother Earth, what he called "death as a social methodology."

Here in these pages, we learn Dan's secret prayer. He has been restored to sanity, to health, to peace of mind and heart and spirit, and prepares to head back to New York City into the turmoil of the world, and, so, he offers up his hope:

> I wish I brought no doubting will
> to clear responsibilities
> I wish a clearer grace
> shone from my face.
> Finally that I might give
> to those of double will
> not reproof, reprieve.

I consider a prophet as someone who takes quality time every day to sit still and listen to the God of peace and then walk out into the culture of violence and war with the message he heard from God—the good news of universal love, universal compassion, and universal peace. The prophet hears and obeys the commandments: "Love one another, love your enemies, put down your sword, beat your swords into plowshares, end your wars, forgive one another, be reconciled, offer mercy, do not be afraid, arise, live in peace with all people and all creation from now on." According to the scriptures, even the Sermon on the Mount, we're called to be a prophetic people, people who seek the God of peace, listen to the God of peace, say what the God of peace says, and do what the God of peace wants. Therefore, we all need a place of peace to listen to the God of peace, restore ourselves to our true selves, be made sane, and send us forth with the good news of justice, disarmament, and nonviolence.

Dan went to Block Island to reclaim his peace, to restore his peace, to return to his center in the God of peace. It was always for him a "Holy retreat," "holy days," as they put it in medieval times—"a holiday" where one attended to body, soul, and spirit so that one would be renewed to carry on one's mission of service to God and humanity.

For Dan, the little house on Block Island, hidden on the cliff, above the ocean, amidst the gulls, became his mountaintop of transfiguration, his holy land of peace, prayer, and healing, his launching pad for resurrection. From there, he lived out his vocation to be a Gospel peacemaker, to be who he was created to be, a beloved child of the God of peace. That was where he prepared for resurrection.

May this collection inspire each one of us to find our own mythic Block Island hermitage of peace, where we rejoin with creation to be renewed in the Holy Spirit and the God of peace, to rise and go forth into the culture of violence and war with good news: that the days of war are coming to an end, that peace is at hand, that we are all the beloved children of the God of peace, and that the invitation to new life and resurrection remains.

BLOCK ISLAND (1985)

THE SEA SHADOWS ITSELF

THE SEA shadows itself, surf like thought
crosses a boundless brow.
The house arose, to look the sea in eye.
Slowly it arose, a child surprised
in a world such—wind, wet, battering storms,
then sun and calm
every mood in the lexicon
and the house enduring, a child required
by harsh stricture, to grow strong suddenly.
Then came friends for healing respite
out of the city's iron clutch
the desperate amenities
of Burial Brigade.
The names kept on the wall
like a votive wall
or a litany of linked loves.
You know them as do I
by heart: scholars, cooks, poets
meditators, for whom sea & land
are one blessing, like the paste
of spit and dirt, an unguent
in the Healer's hand.
House took a chance, as Christian dwellings must
against odds enduring. Weathers opposed
and defects, through which like soul or air
the essence leaked of house.
That was the first delict, from date of birth.
The sea eyed it closely, a gorgon the newborn,

an appetite
a succulent morsel.
Muttered, king of the beasts: I'll inch toward it
I'll have the cliff for first course.

I'VE SAID TO BILL UNEASILY

I've said to Bill uneasily:
dreams in that house are like a hot pot
constantly stirred, fumes intense, voices
grandiloquent. What gives?
Bill, paused between beats, like the sea.
Like the sea, he's no explainer, but pure depth.
He's not on earth to unravel dreams—
to precipitate them rather, like a slowly turned
vintage vat. Drink then, and dream on!

THERE WERE GOOD TIMES AND BAD

There were good times and bad
the absurd mocked us
a polluting wisp from a made stack.
I came & went
friends dwelt here
shaking like water from a
swimmer's pelt, clinging death.
I came again; to join my fate
gradually to theirs;
to proclaim the death of death.
Death: a carcase by charity granted
pauper burial tardy.

THE HOUSE TAUGHT US SHORTLY, RIGHT USE

The house taught us shortly, right use.
I wintered there.
Some grinning sprite
snuffed the fire. Cold settled like a Dickens'
mortician's cloak and hood. Typewriter keys
stuck in its throat. Someone advised: Stick it
in a warm oven fifteen minutes. Sure enough
it resuscitated, gobble-gobbled the next
half frozen turkey page.

SIGNED, SEALED, DELIVERED

Signed, sealed, delivered
my letter to the world
half blotted by sea wind
those surrogate tears
written here, sealed here—
the skin-thin envelope of these walls!
An urban dray horse
out of harness, I was
in my own eyes, next to nothing.
Here I resolved: Be next to
nothing! Shortly
a galling wound healed.

THE NEAREST A JESUIT KNOWS

The nearest a Jesuit knows
of dwelling place. Caravanserai, long house,
urban rooms paid through the nose, shimmy here
shunt there.
Here, sea, land, sky conjoint: with evening fire
a Greek quaternity, reality!

ANTHONY, GREAT BEARDED BEAR OF MAN

Anthony, great bearded bear of man.
At some point
he laid aside use, misuse, urban frenzies
follies, pride of place. Resolved
like a Stonehenge circle, simply
to be. I thought
this deliberately useless man
is image of a useless God.
Teach us so; You who die and live
in the great bearded image of Yourself.

UNEXPLAINABLY, HE DIED

Unexplainably, he died.
Bill, stunned, sought like a good Buddhist
no explanation.
The little house, buffeted, weathered by life
initiated death. We lived on
uncertain as to why, seldom asking;
midst talk, long sorrowing glances a 4 walls
as though the walls dissolved, the dead talked back.

BILL WROTE TO ME IN BERKELEY

Bill wrote to me in Berkeley:
We'll bury Anthony's ashes on your return.
A dazzling dervish nor'easter, rain
striking like blue nails. Bill and I
two faulty frames, dug a small grave.
We lowered the box
no larger than a jeweler's casket shrining
a jeweled time piece. His heart stilled.
Scripture readings, silence.
Hear the rain drum mean time! mean time! the peaceable
echo in nature, of that stilled heart.
Then Bill commanded
in a voice tears and rain together commandeered;
Now we shall face the house; presumptuous death
held sway awhile, shall oust him. We turned
against malignant huff and puff.
And Bill intoned; every jot and tittle
of ancient exorcism. We shivered in our bones
under the driving downpour, prayer books dissolved
to illiterate oatmeal. I thought
what demon worth his salt
would flee comfortable hearth and hutch
for devilish weather?
Dignum et justum. Prayers said,
two hefty islanders
dragged across streaming lawn a four foot whaler's anchor
leaned it crossways over Anthony's grave.
Anchored now. Hope befits
ashes. Anthony anchored above the sea. Hope starts
when worldly hope, flesh, assertive bones
works, pomps, pride, place rule of thumb
religiosities, merits, prevailing clamors, all, all
rendered, reduced, ash. This ash, verily

ash of the body of Christ, humbly melded
with work and clod, shall serve
to save. Anthony, Christ, salvage the shipwreck world.

ABOUT OUR BUSINESS WENT

About our business went, after death's
hiatus, breathing again. The dead were houseled
the living had their house. Grief turned in time
in turning time, to temperate mourning. Pages
by grief defaced, grew legible once more.

IMAGINE ELEMENTS OF THIS HOUSE

Imagine elements of this house—
sun, moon, arc of sky,
humbler creatures, wood, glass, metal, skyey paints.
Recall a 'pre-creation,'
events before the house, events precipitous,
a nosey notoriety intruding. I underground,
friends for only eyes, tapping on walls
our morse code of survival.
It ended here. Freaky bird watchers invaded,
the rara avis snared at last
hauled landward, a smiling slave, stateless,
of holy mother state.
I served (served?)
two years or less in chains
dreaming betimes of chains unstruck,
Block Island like a dreamy hammock hung
between two worlds: Europe, exhausted, dumb
America, colossus unreclaimed.
The house, an uneasy hammock, sways
between worlds. Is it clay of Europe
the sea, the mill of the gods,
grinds to a dust? or America
grinding desperate molars in nightmare?

IT'S NOT MAKING FRIENDS

'It's not making friends
is difficult, but keeping them,'
my father intoned, correct
after the fact, and in person
unverified. Keeping of friends
keeping of house,
learned hardly, late, in pain.
Was it death taught us
drawing us hand in chalky hand
around the hearth, around the bier
processionally?
Lesson 1: in silence
bread rises. 2: sour tongues
spoil the sauce.
3: learn the art
dismiss the dodge; eyes must meet
if friends are not to
turn back, turn away, turn sour.

ISLAND TOO SMALL FOR CONTINENTAL EGOS

Island too small for continental egos; continent too vast
for island souls. I say our souls are islands
contrary to John Donne. We bump and touch
like boats with blind eyes. Crowds
contaminate; not wilfully, in necessity, condemned.
I summon compassion,
the undefeated faces of the subway run
wishing them solitude, this house, cliff,
wild roses, blackberries, scoured pines
the panoply, the subtle dance
self's truth emerging like a headland
when morning fog uplifts a seventh veil.

DAY IN, DAY OUT

Day in, day out
I sought a unifying theme, sought without knowing.
The little house
all eyes, saw for me. I peered through windows
that colored nothing dank or rosy, saw
a waxy bush billowing like a sail; or hunched
face downward, a buffalo riding storm.
No. A mere bush, no burning bush.
Humbled, thankful, hereby I name it.

MUTUAL ISLAND GREETINGS

Mutual island greetings; understated, telegrammatic.
I'd grin like a banshee, riding the jitney to town
passing conveyances, their mode of greeting.
Exuberance, au smit! Not a hand lifted. Anthony gazed
straight on, forefinger barely lifted from wheel's round.
Monotone, monochrome. Landscape, seascape,
befitting gestures. These yankees
know when to leave one alone!
It comes of consonance.
Yankee pizza? More like
cod and dumpling dough.
Go slow, imagine
plagues of tourists,
every quarter year hacked from your side
yourself reduced
to coin squabbling, time serving (your bloodline
whispering of whalers, proud farmers, dissidents.)
Then come back strong!
Reclaim your soul!
smile without bafflement or self betrayal—endurance?

WEATHERED, UNASSUMING, THE CLAPBOARD HOUSES

Weathered, unassuming, the clapboard houses;
their blueprint
is soul's imprint, they weather
as soul weathers, endures. I like that, I greet it
forefinger, so to speak, upraised
to driving wheel of stars and season.

HOW'S THIS FOR TIME WARP?

How's this for time warp?
Years gone, the maladroit
malodorous bird watchers poked about. I sat in the yard
storms gathering, slicing country apples.
They pounced, the bird was nabbed!
That scene, domestic, hilarious, once & for all foreclosed.
Bill gathered 'the remnants, that nothing be lost.'
Two years went by; then
return of the native!
Welcome, spectacular banquet;
Dessert? Resurrected apples,
deep dish pie!

MEMORIES

Memories. Guests at table
noble friends, twice ennobled by death
they sup, depart—
transfigured, undefiled,
down cliffside, turn in farewell.
We saw or thought we saw
them
walking sea waves
away, away, into dawn.

LIFE, DEATH, FRIENDSHIP

Life, death, friendship,
thoughtful and bantering converse,
the house read our thoughts, or thought to,
grew wise before its time. Seasons,
succession of birds; in eaves
like overhanging brows, singing bees,
emblems of survival.

I WRITE THIS SHADOWED BY A TREE

I write this shadowed by a tree
named for Paul's mother Bertel.
Refugee, compassionate to heart's core, so Jewish she was Irish—
'The day Israel took to itself armies and arms,
it was all up with us. I knew.'
We set a small tree
against scouring salt winds. The pine
confounds prediction
flourishing in illustration
of faith's sweet way and will.

INTROIBO AD ALTARE

Introibo ad altare. In the artful parlor
holy Mass. Katherine Breydert
doctor, artist, vivid, mindful, ecstatic
uttered no word save for remembrance
of dead and living souls.
Winter long, her eighth decade, grandly tottering
the unsteady terrain, she ministered to ill & aged.
Frederick brewed on kitchen stove
mastic that set venetian stones; Isaac, Lazarus, Mary
miracles, apocalypse. God's works
her ikon.
One Lent
she forbade visitors, in solitude
suffered the forty days.
Her Easter offering, a child's inspired eye
summoning seven days' creation. These
translated in glass, are glory of Island altar.

THE SCANDALOUS FREELOADING DUCKS

The scandalous freeloading ducks, exempt from law's impeachment
held sway, staggered witless
like drunk sailors, the Breydert roads.
Attacked by lurking underwater predators, the addle pates
hastened to Katherine's ministration.
She splinted broken limbs; the Breydert bath
a Siloe pool, sent them forth healed.

THERE CAME A SEASON

There came a season: Katherine's death.
Cyclic it came, autumn prelude, cold.
Katherine breathed in agony, her meagre need
of prodigal sweet air. Piteous, watching her
like a premature born babe,
laboring, in, out, in—
One autumn, in hospital as usual
(is this the last? we question the last leaf)
I bore an armful of scarlet berried branches
entered her room unseemly, solemn.
Katherine, frail stem of life, propped up
scanning a great Germanic tome of art.
Life of intellect, life of heart
unmitigated. She'd plead, sotto voce:
When I am gone, you will have care of Frederick?

SHE ORCHESTRATED

She orchestrated,
a dying regent, her ambiance.
Anointed, shriven, all in seemly order.
Then Frederick at instrument began
pianissimo, those Mozart themes, half in, half out of our world,
entrance and exit of the spirit's course. Half in our world
she withdrew. A majestic mask lay there.
Mozart diminuendo, she slept. Long life Katherine!

I AM OF AGE

I am of age when grief
is measured by the hollow beat
of shinbones (mine)
against thin-skinned time.
Who dies, and I do not?
Who dies, and I not granted
in that deep-seated loss, some gain,
another advocate?
Katherine, Anthony, Bertel, Tina,
Frederick, John Leary, Stephen, David,
My own parents—
orate pro nobis.

UNEQUIVOCALLY THE SEA SPOKE

Unequivocally the sea spoke. Last night's moony eye
stood witness. For the sea, for God, speech is act.
When we built here, our thought was
(the mystic's outstretched arms, inmost fear)
Near yes, but not too near!
Two fields and more, between us and the void.
The sea, like God, ran counter.
Like wild stallions
sometimes uneasy peace; sometimes barbarian hooves
thrum; danger, danger!
The sea broke fences to a match wood, the sea
foams, roars at doorstep.
What to do?

I KNOW WHAT

I know what. Admit
our real estate
become unreal, our solid ground
illusion, house teetering
at brink. In this obscure
event, unexpected clarity;
the way life goes, between eyeblink and blink—
the beat of providence; I am your only ground.

THE HOUSE SHAKES LIKE A DYNAMO

The house
shakes like a dynamo, the sea
breaks false penates,
intones: No gods here!
Sun burns false ardors to an ash.
Procul este! elsewhere! Else when!
I write this
a three to ten year prison term impending,
the sea a thief of breath, the house and I
terminal patients, reconciled.
Meantime; that strong hand
holds heart in strong hold.
Love; say it
love, the infolded rose.

MEANTIME, ONLY TIME

Meantime, only time. We take readings
from the sun's clock; pure horror.
Midnight, noon? one moral darkness.
'If you could know the hour of your deliverance . . .'
We spread napkins at sea side; the sea gives up its spoils
Swordfish, cod, scallops; eat, be merry.
Hour and hour glass, the Lord walks the waves
mounts the crumbling cliffs of the world
peers in at the wild rose trellis.
At first star
does the world vanish or does He?
If He and not the world
the world's sole meaning is
crumbling cliff. Meantime, our little house unsteady.

A GOOD HOUSE

A good house is one
you send love letters from;
itself good news, standing,
withstanding. More to come.

LABOR DAY

Labor Day. The unlaborious earth
squared off, two distempered camps; employed, unemployed.
Little house, resting on your laurels, your
honeysuckle, wild asters, rose hips
grant us better ways of depoloying
this and that and the corner fruit stand!
Therefore I decree with regal gesture
of bare big toe: No one works today!
Today the very ants put up their feet
the bees grow drunk on capital funds.
Human nature I define anew; unemployed
nay, unemployable! on signal, we shall all
unlearn perverse skills, shall bend our minds—
sweet idleness, sweet Avons,
like a balanced plank on a barrel,
attend the sweet cries
of children;
What else is a mind for?

WHEN THEN IS HOPE?

When then is hope?
not a nail hammered true,
no joist firm without.
Nor could roof sustain
airborne, ceiling bone dry
in driving rain, like spread wing
over fledgling; grace
beyond dumb duty. Fires flare
in face of cold; someone invoked,
someone breathes on behalf.
A large 'meantime' granted against
the world's mad count down. I mean
in all this, hope's many faces.
Then, heart's deep privacy
that keeps and will not tell
fortune, misfortune, all.

GO FROM HERE, VENTURESOME

Go from here, venturesome
knowing not where. A home
is not a tomb. Here Lazarus sleeps
Brief. Then
blazing resurrection.

FRIENDS PAUSE BEFORE A MEAL

Friends pause before a meal
recalling the dead, the absent present travail.
Holy custom assigns
the invisible
more real than things seen.
Therefore no wine sours, no word rankles, the waste of worlds
stops here: modest repast and prayer.

CREATION'S DONE

Creation's done. God
snores away in an armchair in the sky.
(I submit this theological verisimilitude
superior to
pentagon god
multicorporate god
whitehouse cookoo god.)
The old man stirs
the hearth gutters—
He blinks, stands, goes unsteadily to the porch
relieves himself ecologically.
I say, pointing to the cliff: 'Now this
has gone too far.
Another hundred feet to seaward, you and I
find ourselves awash, shortly thereafter
line up for meal tickets and night shelter
at the New York Night Shambles for Men.'
The moon is up; I see refracted
the wolf gleam in his one good eye;
'Do something! the claptrap
comes at me on sixteen winds. do! something!
Anomie raises arm and hammer
to high heaven; the dollar sign
rears like a snake. And I'm supposed
to give the infernal system another chug around!
No go.
I'm on sabbatical. That moldy cliff,
you cope with it—your bad luck, not mine.'

I RECALL, RULING MY THOUGHT

I recall, ruling my thought
Katherine's ikon. Majestic Jesus,
Katherine, fingertips touching
mount a Versailles stairway, court and crown.
No clown.

HERE KEN FEIT DISPORTED

Here Ken Feit disported, who died later.
Command performance, ferry crossing
the children crowding round; a clown
on the ferry! He mimed, cut paper unicorns,
played on kazoos, combs, jews harp—
coast to coast. In Stanford chapel, years gone, Feit and I
made eucharist; he in white face, I in costume
resplendent. The children ran together
at his sweet antic tune.
In wooden pews
the moody regents muttered woodenly.
At recessional this was heard:
'Could Jesus have seen that, he's have
turned over in his grave!'

KEN DIED, THAT SPLENDID GYROVAGUE

Ken died, that splendid gyrovague. His mother, stunned
mandated formal suiting,
a rosary twined in hands. Bill offered
this exegsis: 'Of course, yet
another clown suit!'

PABLO PICASSO SLEPT HERE

Pablo Picasso slept here
offered twelve moony murals, moon shaped girls,
I said, no thank you.
G. Washington slept here,
vanished sans underpants
& upper plate.
I pitched them over the cliff, no shrines here.
Before cock crow, Rockefeller's uneasy ghost
dissolved, absolved, thanks to the Attica dead.
Once only I refused ingress—
an oily character, a dazzling pasteup smile;
'Cement the cliff!' he cried. 'Wrap up the house!
Name your price!
Immediate vacancy, occupancy!'
I spat in his lavender Hollywood eye.
Hustled off, he left a charred footprint.

A GORGEOUS BIRD

Bill said, 'A gorgeous bird
lighted on the crabapple tree
the day you vanished
trussed, manacled like Odysseus
to mainmast for safe passage.'
(I hope that solo act
was my soul doing its thing;
first, last; in any case
unfettered fervent fling.)

I WANDER FIELDS NEARBY

I wander fields nearby
plucking wild sage, mustard, barberry.
And ruminate—
Is this the house
where doubt is exorcised: is this the house
of no betrayal? Our finisterre, the sea
muttering nightlong its witless wild impromptus?
is this the el dorado
of holy fools, who
land failing underfoot
walk water?

DECLAMATORY DAY

Declamatory day; I borrow bad example
from the sea winds that nightlong roistered.
Resolved: a lifeline be laid down
between here and upper Broadway.
Let no one's skull grow grey
until gulls are heard, boisterous and bullying on our pavement.
I want essence of cliff-
and-sea-air blowing past the ear
of aged honorable citizens on busted benches.
Mow down like buttercups the skyscrapers!
this ocean horizon
subtle as eyebrow of Venus on half shell,
must mark straight on, the universal curvature.

THE LITTLE HOUSE UTTERS A NIGHT PRAYER

The little house utters a night prayer:
'Listen to the palms of your hands, the soles of your feet,
the pit of your stomach. You have no other
in such a sea, such world, land mark, sea mark.
For when
by bell, book and candle
they indenture us
to the wheel of ratiocination
we die
like rare beasts in a Freudian zoo.'

THIS HOUSE, THIS HOUSE!

This house, this house! did not fly flimsy to bits
like cardboard in a chimney flare, at Hiroshima.
No children from this porch fled screaming
their frames, frail kites afire
Roses bloom
insouciant, vines unimpeded creep the ground
like limbs of fragrant infants.
All, all is noon-drenched sweetness
courtesy, reward of sense.
Then that shadow
no larger than a hand
that shadow
crosses, double crosses.
Knowing this
we say farewell, kiss our hand
to house, cliff, island. We give over
elsewhere, our days to stern uses
felonious deeds!

BAPTIZED IN CHRIST'S DEATH

Baptized in Christ's death. Water, blood
pour indiscriminate on the little house
which thereupon, like the holy house of Loretto
is rendered fabulous.
Be not astonished
if, on stroke of midnight,
stroke of noon—
table, porch, fundament, roof
pots and pans, with great clatter
levitate in the blue.
Dumb clapboards strike alleluia!
Blue nail heads burn like glass!
Shingles—feathers of birds of paradise!
an angel's shoulder nudges the house, no weightier than
balloon and basket—up, up
into the Presence.

SO IT IS WRITTEN

So it is written. Or so I claim
it is written, roughly the same
when age strips images to bare bone.
Bones of words, bones of hope, bones of a house.
Shall these bones live?

REVELATION ADVISES

Revelation advises
close measurement of a holy place.
I see the seer
on hands and feet, his measure
thrown, and thrown ahead.
Implied
are closure and disclosure;
pacing off, a place
where the world stops short
as though curse or blessing
or both, forbade the freeloading
demons bed and breakfast.

THESIS, ANTITHESIS, BLOCK ISLAND, MANHATTAN

Thesis, antithesis, Block Island, Manhattan.
Tomorrow spins the wheel, I spin
into another orbit, friends, frequencies;
the hellish transport's rebellious roar:
sorting mail, like tugging distant nets ahore.
I wish, I wish.
I wish I brought no doubting will
to clear responsibilities
I wish a clearer grace
shone from my face.
Finally that I might give
to those of double will
not reproof, reprieve.

HUNGER, ANGER, LONELINESS

Hunger, anger, loneliness.
A gull mews, outcries in noon.
I wonder what he sees, walking high
or does not see. I'd
bargain, a trade off, five minutes;
let him pack away at the mind's machine
while I climb for a look on the wind's ladder.

AS THOUGH THERE WERE FUTURE

As though
there were future,
as though
there were God.
Two premises
one; predicament, outcome.
This God I never see
until I forget to look
walking the waves, beckoning.
Until I learn to forget
the unbridgeable void between
that One and me—
I a land creature
can have no hope.

THE LAST DAY

The last day,
this sojourn; which of the real thing
admits analogies; regrets, gratefulness.
They say the last day will strike
monstrous, sucking sea and sy
forever out of amicability.
Analogies;
a gull a hundred feet up, screeched with relief,
crapped! I caught the message
on my intent nose, two chalky drops.

LIKE A SHARECROPPER'S HAIR

Like a sharecropper's hair, the cliff head
shows skull beneath, clipped overgrowth. The skull
invents its shape, like death.
It will turn to me
in moonlight, in sleep, at a gull's intestinal
signal. I taste death hot, full face.

AMERICA

America. If fame evades it's because
you're probably un-American.
Fame: sludge at the bottom of the wine cup.
I want to be famous
only as this house is
to ten or twelve friends
who breathe in its skin;
from its eyes
see on a windy day
an old NY Times dismembered
tumble head over heels away.

RETURN

Return.
Whizzing along, and a voice—
Three minutes to New Haven!
Knowing, new or old
could be no haven—
only a stupendous junk heap
heaving, eructating to high heaven,
as though once and for all,
a tin can culture
gave up the ghost.
University, industry, polity,
the stilled him & whine—
rust and wreck of
stalemated time.

NEW ENGLAND EVENING

New England evening, pools, evening sky
as mother to child, child to mother.
Just now, puffing into town,
a scarred sooty wall—
every cranny
holds like a stone
hand's palm
a tuft, a white autumn flower.
Opposites attract? say rather, life
hangs on, puts out flags.

BIRDS MASS LIKE BEES

Birds mass like bees, the train's
entourage. Then household clearings.
Premature scarlet,
sumac a swipe of blood (that near-tree
of spongy resilience, tree of the poor)
I set down
grief sharpening my sense—
everything John Leary's death denies. Would bring
the round of the world
a wild autumn nosegay, to his grave.

WHO CAN TELL

Who can tell
if discourse or anecdote
make most of truth?
I awake, a form
sits in shadow, birth
or death watch.
Who are the dead, who
the twice born? I cried.
It vanished.
I am left with this
meld of approximation—
death watch of my father,
fields of new children
like pods of autumn, seeding spring.

RARE SPIRIT, RARE

Rare spirit, rare,
Harvard College had not his peer.
'An award for drowning do gooders,' he joked
when honors came his way.
Now a face shines
on water, as though an angel
shone momentary there. And we weep,
letting go.
Memory, keep him,
memory, never the less.
Summon in bread and wine
primary acts. The Lord's death
barely to be borne—
must be, must be. That necessity
I take for discipline, a bell rope
ringing changes, fast, furious
must be! must be! in dead hands.

AND THE SUN SPENDS ITSELF

And the sun spends itself
grandly noon to evening
like creator Spirit
sent into flood
from the Maker's hand
instructed: In mid-sea
make land, make do.

IMAGINE JOHN LEARY CAME

Imagine John Leary came
seeker and seer to this cottage
before the world broke
his untameable heart.
Imagine his short run
ended
at this land's end.
Murmuring his Jesus prayer
at last he new
all that is knowable
thought the world's brutish will
break like sticks or bones
nobles hearts first.
At wit's end, at such ending
of promise, sweetness, surmise
fantasy takes hold—
John Leary at cliff side
life's headlong venture
by no means stalled.
John Leary, child
of air, earth, fire—
his Jesus prayer
come true at last, vision
consumes belief like a straw.
In his element at last
he follows the walker of waves.

THE EMERGENCY MEDICAL TECHNICIANS

The emergency medical technicians
who responded to the call
for help after John collapsed on
a Boston sidewalk were puzzled.
'We weren't sure he was dead
at first,' said one. 'He was
smiling. You don't often see that.'

EIGHTEEN YEARS

Eighteen years. Vocation
came down like a hangman's hood
a last ditch anonymity.
The great experiment!
was it illusion? death wish?
visionary tumble? short change?
Consult the mirror mirror on the wall
of the little house.

DARK ECSTASY BEGAN IT

Dark ecstasy began it.
Hope fueled the miles, furious, slow
a leading voice, overflow,
friendship, friendship; public sense,
words variously judged; but seldom
deceiving, ill tempered, self serving—
cliff, sea, keep counsel.

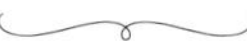

IN DIMINISHMENT

In diminishment
shabby aura of ego dissolves.
We crouch in the out of way
eating our curds and whey.

SOMETHING. MORE.

Something. More.
Now and again heard
in uttermost silence
voice of a summoning bird
tipping the world to innocence.
Gospel moments.
We dwell outside the wall
exiles, without maps.

HANDS, DEAR HANDS

Hands, dear hands
struck flint.
Tom Merton, Bertel, Katherine, Dorothy, Tina,
David, Anthony, John Leary—seeds of fire
made fire, the servitor and sheeted ghost
of the icy world.

DRINKING ONE NIGHT

Drinking one night, Kellerman and I
talked the moon down. 'Think of mad racers
we're at mercy of.
And stuttering engines of air craft
so high the guardian angels peel away—
Then street knifings. And bloody so on.
It's certain we exist
courtesy of bellicose junkers, by merest
suffrance.'
Significant death?
Gold leaf of history, cosmetic
on a split skull.

YESTERDAY, UNUTTERABLE

Yesterday, unutterable
island tragedy.
Two little boys at play
climbed in, slammed the door
of an abandoned ice box
in the weedy yard
of a shingled time worn house.
Mother and father scoured
far and hear, field and town.
The police chief, the rescue squad
cried the names home: Mike! Danny!
like summoning, in contrary wind
sea waves, tides, drowned lambs.
No avail.
Propped in one small box
surrounded on autumn hills
by three hundred islanders, banal death
has its day.
The Baptist minister weeps
invoking numina of faith
mothers, merchants, sailors, stevedores
sway like reeds
in rude storm.
Once on a time, children perished
otherwise—spectacular at sea
or tumbled over monstrous cliffs
or by witch's wiles brought low—
seized by the great fist of fate
that savage sibyl, that claw and claimant,
that hand from a muttering cloud.

NO MORE

No more. It is junk yard death
rusty death
death the recusant, the coward
the undoer of children.
No legend accrues
as of plagues, dervishes, ghosts at dawn
cities evaporated
torturers racking the human frame
stretching the soul's measure.
No. Craven weak kneed death
death the cliché, literal toothy death
let us amid tears, despise.

AT THE CHILDRENS' FUNERAL

At the childrens' funeral
women wept free, men
like camouflage of mourners
stood stiff among the stones
(for honor, for balls, for America)
One gesture redeems all!
The young mother, tragic, bowed
like a grandmother crone
(that hour's pitiless blow)
placed a rose o the white box,
a wraith, withdrew.
Then all were summarily dispersed
by a silk-suited official face.
The rose, the box, ourselves
suspended
in mid air, mid gesture
amid the mounds of
dead mortician grasses
And the dead children
not yet dismissed
lay like dreamers, frozen in dream
in surmise, in limbo, in tears withheld.
Then in vision, I tossed a great dark clod
upon their prison. Dust
to dust! I yelled. And the children
laughing, mounted
dolphins
bounding
elsewhere.

AS THOUGH OCEAN HORIZON

As though ocean horizon
were a quick sand,
a big cumbersome cargo's
stuck out there.
It takes the vector
of eye & sun & time, to measure that
infinitesimal progress, a burdened
sea slavey laboring the world's cage.
Philosophically inclined, I mutter:
Life's like that
best scuttle cargo
and stoke a steadier beat
in the mortal engine.
Theologically inclined
I sit tight, a regurgitated
Jonah, humming: Near, my God . . .
Only
barely
Davy Jones' locker
falls short of hell.

IT WASN'T STRIVING

It wasn't striving
counted for much, it was
play, interplay, dovetailing;
The gulls' cake walk & take off
achieving with minimal brain power
marvels of grace. Aloft, the birds walk
like God-intoxicated ghosts
an extra gospel mile,
winds' graceless rebuff
not rebuffed in turn
but beckoned, welcomed, packed in!
Wings hunched, birds put on the wind
like sleeves of gown or great coat
Then roll the wind
like a newspaper under arm
carried home.
Home. Believe it, good news!

BE CONSOLED, BARRISTER

Be consoled, barrister. In life
intricate law binds tight. In death
the law's fetters
hold even dry bones in escrow.
Norma, sharp tongued elegant drunk
expired at length, of frequent
infusions of unspeakable fire waters—
hair tonic, throat garble.
The law's long
necrophilic tooth
harrowed her grave. The law
beat like a cop's night stick on her
impervious midnight lodging.
But she (princess grown canny
with many a cadge & bilk & ploy)
vanished by secret
postern door
revved up her ghostly taxi
dispatched an imperious rune
by mortal hands of mournful Little John:
Varmints, depart my premises;
I am
not
here

NIGHT FALLS

Night falls. The sleepy fire sputters, ruminates
like a dreaming dog.
Bones shift in sleep. One red eye
closes like a log.

DANIEL: GOD IS MY JUDGE

Daniel: God is my judge.
Names I've been named, post baptismal
would bulge a bad cess album.
One said: You're an easy rider.
Another: Straw man.
Another: Alas, depressed spirit.
I like Tina's. She let it marinate for months:
'I don't call you hero, that's too easy.
Nor saint, that's too soon.
I call you messenger. And refuse to die
until I hear the message.'

Daniel: God is my judge.
Like being born legless in a pot hole.
Biology, destiny.
But why so many preludes, I fret,
to the Big Conclusive Act? why these interminable
out of town openings?
We tried the
tragico-comico-farce in
New York, Washington, Baltimore, Arlington, Norristown
Also in Berkeley and L.A.—
everywhere the hammer came down, triphammer of time—
GUILTY!
In re, yr. honor, I am led to ask
what the hell connection obtains here
with the Big Finger of Matthew c. 25?
Are we bucketed blind Greeks
spinning willy nilly in gyres of fate?

And the Cocks of the Walk in snoods & shrouds
that conceal the silken suits
that conceal the bones dry bones—
are they
in short, the Only Gods, as claimed?
OR
will the real one
lurking perchance in our unfortunate alleys
please come forward?
(Now and then, what someone saw
or thought she saw—
'That ragged figure, flitting from tree to tree
in the back of the mind.'

THE LUXURY, THIS PLANK PORCH

The luxury, this plank porch
like a raft bobbing in shallows
this million dollar
prospect: me
king of the raft, grandly setting down lines
like life lines to the dead.
Sitting, sitting, a broad based Buddha
where life lines converge; or
a camp fire the dead creep toward
to warm their hands.

WHERE POLITICS LURCH TO A STOP

Bill says: where politics lurch to a stop, compassion starts.
I think politics end where politics start;
i.e., someone primordially pissed on the dynamite.

NOWHERE TO LAY HIS HEAD

‘Nowhere to lay his head,’ I recall wryly
laying me down in this house.
History’s rule of thumb, thus verified:
‘Things go as they go, they rightly go,
ethics arise from property, not vice versa.’
I wonder what a troop of motley fools & sages
at large in the countryside, might—

WE CAN'T THROW A SHAWL DOWN THE STEEP

We can't throw a shawl down the steep.
The clay won't grow its own hirsute
more than a sere skull hair;
no awakening nature to pity our house.
In Peru they toss a stuck pig
over an endangered bridge
into the torrent, they say it works.

THE FIRST HOUSE

The first house was in Ely Minnesota.
We packed its foundation
every October with two foot banks
of dry foliage: otherwise no surviving
Ol' Blaster. I remember, I remember
tin washtub athwart the stoop
talisman of the poor,
a big drum drumming my mother's
indenturehood.
Indians in birch bark canoes
beat the lake shore for wild rice.
Winter night, wolves
howled the moon up over Moose Lake.

SPEAKING OF WOLVES

Speaking of wolves. Winter day
lucid as a diamond's heart. Brother
hoisted me to shoulder outdoors
in sparkling cold. Into the wood shed.
Blinded, I sensed a hairy phiz
pushed against mine. Little boy's
eyes cleared, through darkness stared—
baleful moons, a stark suspended
timber wolf, frozen, eye to eye.
Screamed and screamed!

SOME BREAD RISES

Some bread rises, some
squats there, mere avoirdupois.
Generational penury
broke like a clay mold, long fired, cooled, fired.
We broke through to what might be called
in defiance of dread and dream—
mitigated tragedy.
Stand at the mirror,
glance with undisfiguring eyes—
a face fused in a crowd
a clerical joe or joke, credentials
altogether negative, to wit:
neither blind deaf dumb
Therefore;
I shall say what I see, and
more than a bundle of blind sticks
shall walk in directions commended
by ancient guides. The dead.

DANGER

Danger.
What to make of that ambulant
island, sane Jesus?
He peddles from his pack; forgiveness, healing.
Derides code, taboo, rite,
seasons, moons, incantations.
Attend. Read in the intimate heart
a bill-board back-packed
among the mad: 'Repent; be made
sane!'

FOURTH OF JULY, DANBURY PRISON

Fourth of July, Danbury prison. The prisoners
turned out for fun & games.
The unincarcerated weather
called halt to the mad charade, raining dismay.
But prisoners will be prisoners, to the wall.
The keepers, keeping time, yelled:
'Run for cigarettes, run for cokes, run for your lives!'
So they ran; mechanical hares chased by
official dogs.
But if prisoners duly run
they run not far. The lead hares
through veils of rain and mud, slammed face first
into blank wall. Briefly
rain
ran
red.

IN JUGGERNAUT AMERICA

In juggernaut America
all willy nilly ride,
all, willy nilly, pay.
In whatever coin.
Here comes, speaking of,
our ticket-taker now.
Why, sir, the damp brow?
chalk hands? averted eyes?
Are you someone else, mayhap, in disguise?

IN THE ISLAND SANCTUARY

In the island sanctuary
hierophant and sycophant contend.
Whom worship? The Christ blazing wordlessly
from windows that like eyes see, are not seen through?
or the ranting redwhiteblue of the flag
flaccid at altarside?
The priest purses his lips
temporises: 'Why not both
postulates, realms, lords?'
July fourth, he wraps
shivering Jesus in imperial shroud, hustles him
in a tumbril through the town. Parody,
pomp, circumstance, riddled with death.

THEY ALL BLEW AWAY

They all blew away
like candles out of doors;
someone saw a wolf's head at the window
the night hurricane Guernica
reeked and raved

All blew away
not one saved

Because the wolf's head talked
back, back in its throat
they hurried for a priest
who swore it said distinctly
Follow Me!

They impaled the head on a broom.
In the priest's hands
it grew loquacious, avuncular.

Upstreet and down
they follow the death head
in the dark town.

Now they have a savior
and not one sign.

A PORCH FACING THE SEA

A porch facing the sea
September noon, late summer haze receding.
Like a dazed microbe, over a microscope
I'm ferreting out Greek scripture,
word for word. Wonderful!

TODAY, PLUCKED A SACK OF CRAB APPLES

Today, plucked a sack of crab apples
set them boiling in honeyed juices;
sweet, sour, native to the time
honeyed autumn time,
every weed still and sane.
Under leaves a shadow whispers:
ruin, shortly, begin.

TOMORROW THIS HOUR

Tomorrow this hour, I'll be
pounding macadam, a ragged insect
zigzag to his hive.
Autumn thrums the life span's
abrupt quietus.
Shall works be sternly judged
even insect works?
Disconsolate I wander,
hardly wing.
Have mercy, fiery angel, son of man.

ADDITIONAL POEMS

The little front room of Dan's cottage: kitchen counter, bookshelves, bathroom door, bedroom door, desk, and wood stove. Behind was a little dining table. The large stone mosaic under the counter is "The Raising of Lazarus" by islander and Dan's friend Katherine Breydert. Photo by John Dear.

A good house is one
you send love letters from;
itself good news, standing,
withstanding. More to come.
D. Berrigan (1985)

MY FRIENDS, IT IS THE SAVOR OF LIFE

My friends, it is the savor of life
you passed to me; vines, the diminished loaf
lost hillsides where the sun
set the grapes beating like a hive
of human hearts; Cornell gorges, the distant sea
Block Island swung like a hammock from its moorings—
I come to myself
a beast in a shoebox

Daniel Berrigan, from "WE WERE PERMITTED TO MEET
TOGETHER IN PRISON TO PREPARE FOR TRIAL"
(*Prison Poems*, 1973)

COTTAGE INDUSTRY

I thought to sing aloud a simple poem quaker or shaker
noislessly twirling separatist, sexless the world
a waxed floor showing us back heel to head, a theology, anthropology
from below No, such complexities, what a fond fool;
We spin like spiders glances like cables eye to eye
The web sways, sings like a trampoline anchored in souls,
thump thump it goes under the hobnails.

Published in *The Works*, a Block Island arts journal, July 1995, page 42.
(Courtesy of Carolyn Brown and *The Works*.)

DAYS ON AN ISLAND IN JANUARY WILL DO THIS TO YOU

Sun, moon, storm
Nothing last
Nothing should, they say in the city
Whose clocks run fast, run past
Like people.
Yesterday snow owned the yard like a pall on a dead face
Slowly drawn
Imagine you saw the snow ever so slowly draw breath an inch or two above the face
You were so close to who just went
You hardly breath.
The walls, stone walls
Big stones, each a guard
Facing, if so a face, facing away.
Today, thawing snow creeps close, curved, cold as a serpent's lip
For survival
A thin white line, then a dark line,
Impressionists caught it,
Careless and caring
The shadow of stone owns like God
All that barely makes it this far.
And out at sea,
Waves a league long arrive from Portugal
And die like near-heroes ashore
Spectacular!
They resemble the pharaoh's chariots, horses, and men tumbling down
Scriptures, expendables, watery warriors
Another, then another
Tries, and dies.

Obsessed, you say?
Give them credit!
That willfulness marching straight up the cliff
To return you, every one of you
Back, the pharaoh barker,
Back where you belong.

—Daniel Berrigan, John Dear, ed., foreword by Bill Wylie-Kellermann, *The Trouble with Our State* (Resource Publications, 2021).

FIVE SENSES OF THE END TIME

1.
When I look back I see
I've spent my life seeing—
under that flat stone—what?
why that star off kilter?

Turn turn, I intoned, and
out of the stone there stood
What-Not in a white garment.

Jacob's ladder descended
(the angels holding steady)

I mounted and I
saw what

2.
What then did you hear?
(a rabbi intoned on the way)
'Death knell, birth cry, both
wrung from throat.'

3.
Taste was gruesome and sweet.
First, a prison privy.

They pushed your face down
in the common woe of war,
the shit of conquering heroes.
But then in a desert place

honey from a lion's jaw!
I tasted at long last

alleluia!

4.
In no time at all
death, and you're compounded
princeling or jackanapes
with common carrion stench.

Which isn't the point I believe.

I carry in memory
like a bride her bridal flower
in two tremulous hands—
odor of wild roses
wet with Block Island fog.

5.
It was touch and go all the way.
I saw along the way
blur of blood, then closer
a wounded wayfarer
hands, feet, heart's pocket
rent savagely.
Touch! he cried, and live!
Mirror mirror—
him I saw, myself
rent. And in went.

—Daniel Berrigan, published Sunday, October 15, 2000, in Agni, volume 52.

HORTICULTURAL NOTE

I sign of New York roses.
Despite instruction scrupulously observed
(stems cut, blooms immersed in water)—
do not open their arms like water angels
or angels of annunciation
saying for all the world's sake—
Believe us, winter is ended!

No, they pant and droop
like poor families on fire escapes
on awful July nights, when the sun
a furnace, leaves behind
for only sunset, live coals of a furnace.

I will now account for the above.
To wit, New York roses are not New Yorkers.
They are like buddhists in exile,
they are everywhere elsewhere
in mourning for a sunrise
the buddha holds forever
secret, aloft
a third eye, for them only.

—Daniel Berrigan, originally published in *The Works*

DEATH AND LIFE OF A FRIEND

My last death was William Stringfellow's.
Death
rattled its begging bowl
like the drummer of Armageddon.
Sustenance! Sympathy! it drummed

Stringfellow bethought; Death
lacking a name—
(Unnameable, nameless horror
they muttered in terror)—
he named it finally, taming
once for all
the appetite that fed
on kings and clowns—
fed and fed, never satiated—
women, warriors, the sleepy eyed unborn—
never enough!

We must break this thrall
once for all, became his mind's
holy obsession and vocation.

Like a priest's crucifix aloft
before the obscene undead,
Christ expiring for love, summoning a last
commanding cry; Down dog death!—

Thus Stringfellow. Transfixed, laid claim
years and years, a crucifix in hands
not his, miraculous he moved in the world
chasing death pitilessly
dismaying, dispelling death.

Then as the sun advances, and shadows
go underground
he stands, believe, in resplendent noon.
Taken from the cross
he ascends straight up.

And death, shadowy, starved, named
for what it is, is not
and no where to be seen.

—Daniel Berrigan, published in Sojourners magazine, December 1985

YOUR SECOND SIGHT

(for Philip)

Walking by the sea
I put on
like glasses
on a squinting
shortsighted soul—

your second sight

and I see
washed ashore
the last hour of the world—

the murdered clock of Hiroshima.

—Daniel Berrigan, from Bill Wylie-Kellermann's *Celebrant's Flame: Daniel Berrigan in Memory and Reflection* (Cascade Books, 2021).

1.

BLOCK ISLAND

Seeing the gulls
spontaneous
erupt over the headlands
hover there
like paper in a flue
while the hoarse constant tide
gathers, dies ashore -

The Greeks
wrote of 'spontaneous generation'
warriors from dragons' teeth
(alas, our world
mined for apocalypse) -

spontaneous
the gulls'
generation over the headlands

'And my word shall return to me' -

hoarse, witless, witnessing
the gulls, the sea -

not prophets, prophecy.

2.

BLOCK ISLAND

Walking by the shore
I put on
like glasses on a squinting
shortsighted soul -

your second sight

And I see
washed ashore
the last hour of the world -

the murdered clock of Hiroshima.

3.

BLOCK ISLAND

A last look at the sea
like a last look at earth

or a face weeping
or a tolling bell
for our going

Where we come from
we know at the end
or too late -
except ...:

we turn
(that face, that sea)
and shall know.

HY-IR FOR YALL A POME FROM B.I

Seeing the gulls
in great flocks spontaneous
erupt over the headlands
like paper in a flue
while the hoarse constant tide
gathers, dies ashore -

The Greeks
spoke of spontaneous generation
warriors from dragons' teeth.
Alas our world
mined for apocalypse -

Spontaneous
the gulls'
generation over the headlands
'And My word shall return to me'.
Hoarse, unlikely, witless, witnessing like the sea
not prophets, prophesy.

AFTER ROME, ASSISI, FIRENZE, RAVENNA, DUBLIN, CONNEMARA, ETC, ETC.

HAPPY SCHOOL OPENING!! ♡ DANIEL

Daniel Berrigan, Poem from B.I., c. 1981. Jerome C. Berrigan papers, box 6, folder 1. Special Collections and Archives, DePaul University Library, Chicago, IL.

PHOTOS

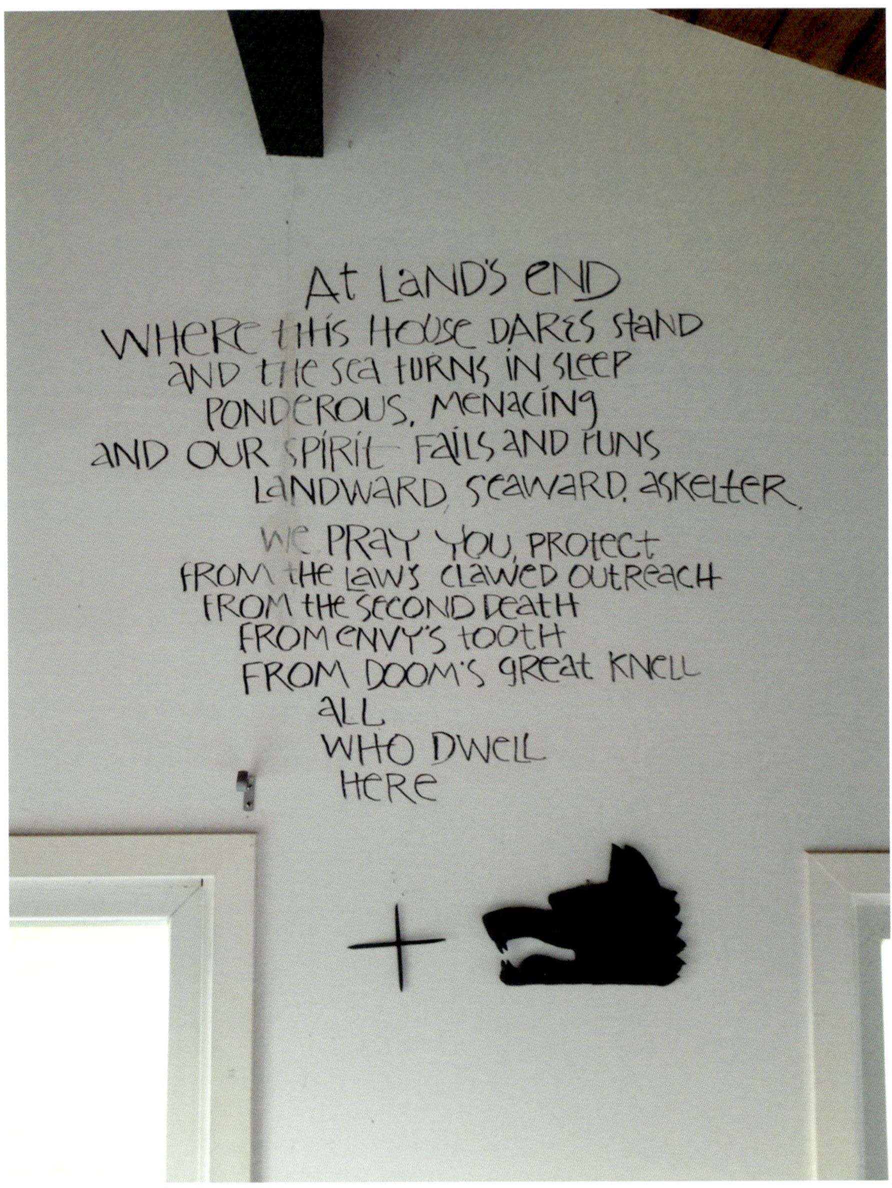

The poem which Dan painted with black ink by hand on the wall of the cottage. (Photo courtesy of John Dear.)

A view of Dan's cottage from William Stringfellow's house.

The cottage. (Photo courtesy of John Dear.)

Dan reading a book on the top of the BI ferry as we made the crossing one day in the late 1990s.

Dan and Bob Keck.

Steve Kelly, Dan, and Bob Keck.

Mary Donnelly and Dan on Main Street.

Dan on the BI ferry.

Dan on the deck of the cottage.

Dan coming out of the cottage to greet John Dear as he arrives one morning.

Bob Keck, Dan, Mary Donnelly, and Steve Kelly on Main Street.

Watercolor of the cottage by Jessie Edwards.

Dining table in the corner of the cottage, and the decks looking out over the ocean.

Dan on the deck of the cottage.

The day of William Stringfellow and Anthony Towne's burial.

Another view of the cottage deck.

John Dear and Dan on the BI ferry.

Watercolor of the cottage gifted to Dan. Artist unknown.

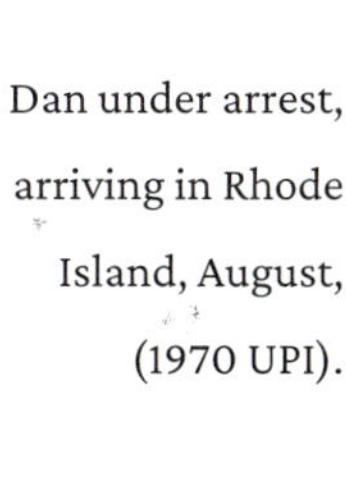

Dan under arrest, arriving in Rhode Island, August, (1970 UPI).

Jim Wallis and Bill Wylie-Kellermann digging the grave for Stringfellow.

(Photo courtesy of Scott Kennedy.)

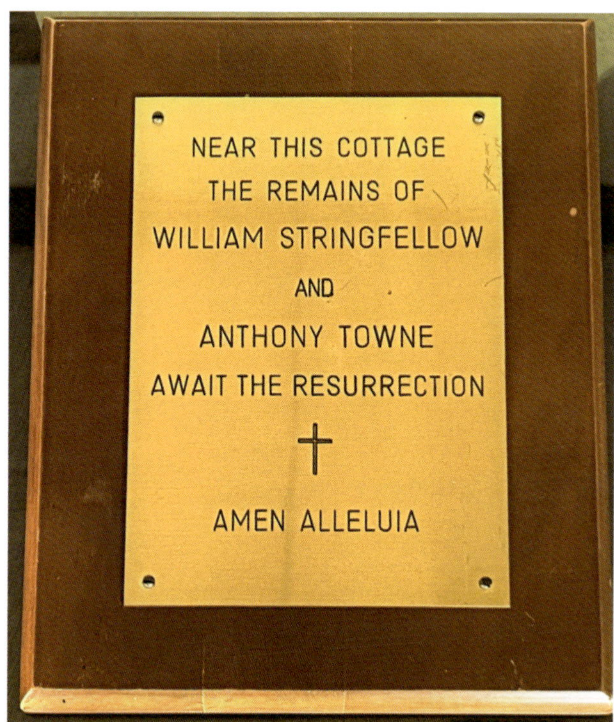

Memorial plaque designed by Dan for the burying of William Stringfellow's ashes.

Dan back on the mainland in the hands of FBI agents.

LETTERS

Dear Bill, Jean, chilluns, 21 March

Such good news that you'll all be descending on the Blessed Isle come May!

And thanks so much for sending on the splendid book to Bill McNichols. I prob'ly added the Sojourner folks are shipping on photos as well. I can't but think that in the proffer of an ikon of Bill we have something providential in our hands. Handle with care!

I wanted also to urge that you, Bill, have something a bit more defined to do with the Saturday occasion. You sit an interesting cockpit, what with months and months of immersion in the Stringfellonian mystique.

What hath God wrought? I venture it'd be of great interest to all in attendance, were you to speak words, chiefly concerning your work on the biography, how it's affected views on everything from family to teaching to the imbedded, socialised misery (which Bill with third eye wide, saw coming, saw arrived; and which by now (O lucky man, to be out of it all!) is a foul political staple), to community, to resistance, to prayer and worship, to illness & death.

I venture someone of your tenderness and intelligence finds affinities and learning and cause for much pondering in this work. I venture too that talk of such matters would be of great solace and back bracing to the embattled friends.

Anyway. Does the above strike a chord, set the heart ringing?

Fondly, all of yez.

14 December

Dear Bill,

Blessed holiday to you & yr dear ones!!!!! I pray that even the famous bushwacker may find a tear or two to anoint the graves of Iraqui children this Christmas......

And so many thanks for the good enclosures. The writings are like a hot sunrise out of a grave. What a thunder in the midst of the softsoap & hard nosed bullshit we commonly are afflicted with from 'church'!

I thought of the Graham intro being immediately published in say, Sojourners. This in view of the latest defection of the famed one, straight as a smart bomb, into the Gulf war blessing. Whaddye think?

As to the Winsome intro, and the drawings, I'm of course intrigued. But equally of course, wd. have to have more of the drawings at hand to dream dreams over. Bill & Tony had one or two of Benes on their wall, invariably witty and ping! to the point. Do you advise my getting directly to the Cornell curator?

There is an entire Bill-Ben Nordberg saga; do you know of it? Ben and wife (at whose funeral Bill preached a hair raising homily that had the pews in co;nsiderable turmoil) owed Bill big money for legal affairs. After her death Bill went to the house & piled his car with goodies, antinques etc. I could tell more; the wife is commemorated in a poem or two in the Block Island book.

Well I hope the new year brings you (and by strong implication, usns) closer to having the S'fellow works back on shelves, in hands & pulpits & convents & missions & even right adjacent to toilet bowls (where B. often did extensive reading.....

Love to y'all from us all.

So many thanks too for 'Witness', which I hadn't seen since the move. Do you ever take articles? (i.e., from 'unknown divines')

Daniel

Christmas Day –

Dear brother –

I'm tardy as usual, but many fond thoughts go in your (and family's) direction, with hopes that Jonah community flourishes, with you aboard, in '89. Also hopes for Holy Innocents' witness, and your and Liz's trial!

Now that we have a wedding date, we can look forward to a N.Y. meeting of the clan.

Please thank Martha (I lost her address!) for sending on the fine '89 calendar.

I have no word from our chimney repairman, no bill. Did you get one? has the work been done?

All warmest,

Daniel

Dear bro Jimbo, 30 Jan. '96

I presume by now you're ensconsed in the Cottage of Clairvoyants, and that all goes well there, the kettle & the heart humming softly hymns of beatitude.

Bob said you and he had some good palaver & viands. Wish I'd bin there, even a bug on the wall, all ears for years. (Poetry)

I'm so glad you're to have the place for these three months. After all, you've been the prime mover in all the great developments of the house & grounds - down to the downing of the last wee mousie in the wainscoting!

Hope too the solitude and peaceableness of the place will bring enlightenment on your next move.

The wonder continues. So many great folk have found refreshment and a new start there; even though the 'start' was proceeding through the midnight unknown of AIDS, or jail time, or even death. God keep our dear Mev!

You and I held palaver one evening as to tasks that needed attention. I remember the following;

- servicing of kerosene unit
- cleaning stove & stove pipe
- replacement of fallen drain pipes (presently under deck)
- (toward end of April) replacing screens
- (I guess next summer) replacing boards on deck, resurfacing deck.

I'd be happy of course, to go halves on any expenses involved.

It's always a joy to think of you as podner of the place, where your skills are in shining evidence all over.

Sure hope the yoga classes are crowded.

John Marth gave a report to Kairos last Tuesday. He's doing heavy labors on the birthday party May 4. I told the group of your kind offer to come and survey the Xavier facilities and help with menu. John said he'd call you.

Ned left for Philippines last Sunday.

This Saturday I wing off to Salvador and Guatemala. Please send a prayer. I'll give your warmest to John.

Love to the beloved & yourself, to parents, all other friends (I'm such a dolt on names).

Enclosed a few goodies from Ben, Jerry and

Daniel

WAS MADE TO UNDERSTAND ON THE PHONE THAT THE local priest would do the ceremony. However on my arrival, a good 40 minutes late on the dratted amtrak, it was shortly announced that I was the clief guru. Did me best.

Tommy announced that he and Virginia went looking for John in Ely and came on him & had a good talk, also that John's in good fettle, though mourning the $.50 cups of coffee in that berg. Well, if that's all his trouble!

Bill is in fine shape, brown as Gandhi in July, I've been reading his book Wich does seem to me his best yet.

It's been cloudy but not chilly. The tourists in plague numbers, look dehydraded & unready for America...

I saw the Breydert windows. And wonder of wonders, as I was pointing out the B. house to Jim Wallis, who departed today, we went up to the house to see if we could

Daniel Berrigan to Dears, August 31, 1981. Jerome C. Berrigan papers, box 6, folder 1. Special Collections and Archives, DePaul University Library, Chicago, IL.

view any of the art through the windows. Found a door wide open to the elements, all the art untouched, we had a full spate of (for me) unbearably vivid memories and for him, first sight of the mosaics. I see I've run out here, except for much love & thought of all..

♡ Daniel –

start here

31 August 1981

Dears,

Tonight Bill & I et off the new table. Scrumptious (if I have the word right); at least everything, including Carol's bean casserole, tasted as tho Venus had risen in a shell, meal in hand, from the sea. How's that, Ma?

Anyway. Just to say I arrived in fine fettle, borne to the ferry by Tom, Virginia and Briget. Who still calls Tommy 'daddy'. Frank of the handlebar mustash, is still much in evidence, chic & handlebarred as ever. B. sez he's made it big in a new disco bar he opened a year ago, graced by a life sized statue of his nibs, in wood, hand done by a friend, handlebarred & all! So there.. Big Bruv in hearing all these wonders recounted, maintains a discreet if not aggrieved, silence. Virginia, I imagine, though I didn't check in the rear view mirror, can be thought to lower her eyes.

Liz is loverly as an August peach. She was a bit dissheveled as to the décolletage, I ast if this was the layered look, she said, No it's a Mexican wedding dress. One thing about Liz like her mother, you can allus get a straight answer to a ditto question.... The young un is just back from Minnesota, great outspoken gal, and she anddaddy seem (drat it) to make it better.

It was also typical of this informal crowd, that I

GREAT HAPPINESS
GRAND BONHEUR

Art populaire traditionnel Vietnamien
au profit des réfugiés et victimes de guerre au Vietnam
Délégation de Paix de l'Eglise Bouddhique Unifiée du Vietnam
11, rue de la Goutte-d'Or, PARIS-XVIII° (France)

Daniel Berrigan to Dears, August 31, 1981. Jerome C. Berrigan papers, box 6, folder 1. Special Collections and Archives, DePaul University Library, Chicago, IL.

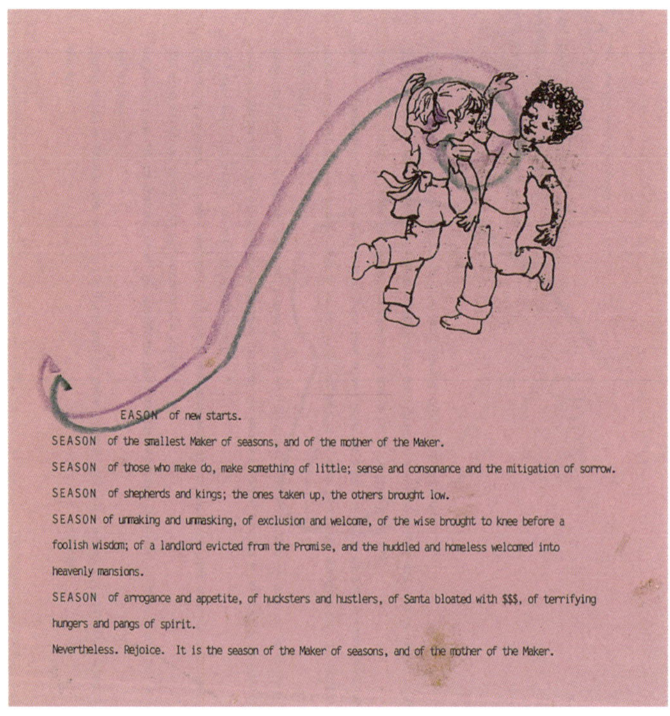

SEASON of new starts.

SEASON of the smallest Maker of seasons, and of the mother of the Maker.

SEASON of those who make do, make something of little; sense and consonance and the mitigation of sorrow.

SEASON of shepherds and kings; the ones taken up, the others brought low.

SEASON of unmaking and unmasking, of exclusion and welcome, of the wise brought to knee before a foolish wisdom; of a landlord evicted from the Promise, and the huddled and homeless welcomed into heavenly mansions.

SEASON of arrogance and appetite, of hucksters and hustlers, of Santa bloated with $$$, of terrifying hungers and pangs of spirit.

Nevertheless. Rejoice. It is the season of the Maker of seasons, and of the mother of the Maker.

Dear Bro Jimbo, November 20, 1 9 9 1

Yr. faithful servant reporting in, midst of national turmoil, inner tranquility, Bush-wacking endured cheerfully day upon day at hands of abovementioned eminence in wicked league with cooonspirator against humanity, nempe General Schwartz-dumkopf.

Well, and hoping yr. the same.

As to the cottage, and wondering if yr. plan to venture islandward during winter season, is still aloft & starry???

As to above celestial dwellilng; Bob Keck, last resident of fading season, accomplished the following;

- help of a willow wand or like bewitchery, came upon buried honey pot, so to speak, uncovered same to high heaven, called honey-pot-emptier. Who on the hour voided same of precious essence of 20 some years of gourmet cookery. Ahem. Same basic Bob paid for service; 150 smackeroos.

- likewise; installed lock on door. Removed and stored screens. Brought plank & box desk indoors. Summoned someone re pilot light & turned off same. Likewise, I presume, courtesy of yr. mother, water off.

- to think about; bed sityaashun, lousy. Also improvement of main installed bookshelves, to include larger books. Also bookshelf ladder of sorts.

David & Goat are paid in full. I wrote urging a final clearing along south wall, lest we lose effects of gargantuan herculean labors of the summer.

I guess that's that, for now.

Are you thriving?

I miss yr. spontaneous zest, skilled hands & munificent heart. Come to the apple.

Daniel

Dear Ned, Scott, Jim Wallis, Jim Reale, January 12, 1 9 8 9

I'm sending along to Ned Hastings, a bill for chimney repairs recently completed on the Block Island cottage.

The bill is an honest one, detailed as to items of work and material. It amounts to $535.11.

There was no putting off the work, we were warned. Or if it were put off, the bill would be doubled by spring time.

Unfortunately, due to taxes, lawn mowing, power, gas, phone, and other evidences of mortality, the cupboard here is bare. Therefore this note. I hope the estate can take care of the matter. If not, we can disassemble the chimney and notify Santa there's no use stopping here.

That's the bad news; the good is, blessed and newer year. Despite all.

Gratefully,

Sorry the courts (as usual) played Herod. You're the stronger for it.

We'll see where this tactic (letter + bill to Hastings) lands. What the hell, we have nothing to lose!

Are you OK?

Bob + Beloved due here tomorrow, wedding bells —

A.M. arrests at Riverside " . Martin Sheen'll be w. us.

to all there, Daniel

"You're a mystic, Mr. Ryan. All Irishmen are mystics."

Dear Jimbo, Friday 18 June.

Just great to be with yez at the John Dear celebration & late at night at Jonah. Good talk, wonderful food, you at yr. best!!!!

I had a minor brainstorm about the cottage. Have no idee what yr. work day is like or whether there's a chance to do a bit of carpentry there..... What I thought of was a bookcase against the wall, over the door to the bedroom; this one with large spaces for large books, to relieve the other smaller units.... There isn't all that time to work in the empty place, as I have on the calendar that John Dear arrives (with y;ou?) just after the Stringfellow weekend. But just a thought.....

Well my affectionate best to yrself, mother & dado & Annie. Alas for Zoe.

Dan B.

Sermon on the Mount (Mt. c. 5)

23 Sept—

Dear bro Jim—
Good news on Groton outcome. So many thanks for phoning.
This is just 2 say there are books galore here by D.B., including some 20 copies of <u>BI Poems.</u> And others as well. I don't know if Glass Onion folk want to 1) take some now or 2) wait till Spring. (Or if the BI poems were best offered for sale at the po'try reading?)
By the way I have marked <u>Oct. 23</u> for the reading. Is this firm?
Only hitch in the book situation is getting them transported to the Island. Any ideas?
You may want to discuss above with Lyn also, regarding books.

love + gratitude—
Daniel.

I await news on
baleful foundation-cottage $.
Pray for Ned Hastings!

KAIROS PLOWSHARES TWO

In this hour ('kairos') of crisis and opportunity
we, the 'Kairos Plowshares Two
attempt to carry the Plowshares Process further
to continue to free ourselves from the paralyzing power of fear
fear of failure, fear of courts and prison, above all, fear of powerlessness
- to walk to the Trident D-5 missile tubes and symbolically disarm one
- to name it with our own blood.

Kathy Maire, OSF
Anne Montgomery, RSCJ

August 1, 1988
Quonset Point, R.I.

Friday

Jimbo dear bro—
I couldn't put foot down in this blessed spot without thinking of and thanking for, all you've done to make & create and imagine. Everything is in good

form after the Wallis' left, I bin layin low
So far just like brer Rabbit. But Mary D. and
ol' croneys (cronies?) will gather. Full o' the
moon! And we'll crack a jar for yez too!
I caught Tom Mitchell + paid him $260.
He sed he'd send you the bill already. Disregard.
He talks about yet another go, but I think he
has FINN'S SUBURBIA in mind. I hope you'll tell
him thass snuf 4 this season!
Your mother, Kindness herself, picked me up at
airport + delivered same 2 land's end.
Plenty vodka on hand. I've took 2 mixin' it
up, batch after batch. In the bathtub. So nice 2
wallow in, bettern' Cleopatra's bath of mare's milk.
Well, I'll see y'all, Deity willin, when Phil's
out at last, 15th. Please much

off the page, to
Y'all. Daniel

Dear Jim + John 22 July –

This is a quick stirrup cup on the way practically to the airport, to thank both of you for recent letters, and to hope the injustice system is showing some unwonted mercy... one hopes on. We've seen bigger mis-carriages of justice, but seldom something so overtly brutal. My prayers to to John and friend, even as I wing out for London.
Jim, heartfelt thanks once more for the fine work on the cottage.
All sorts of people are going to be in debt for a long time, to your skills and devotion. Thanks to you on behalf of all of them - and me most of all.
It looks like a heavy week ahead, but good folks.
I'm thinking much of Phil also,~~and~~ the others,and the sentencing.
Parlous times, good good folk, our blessing.
Yall be well, I hope to see you soon after arrival - and we'll crack a jar. Love to everyone in the ho;use.

Dan

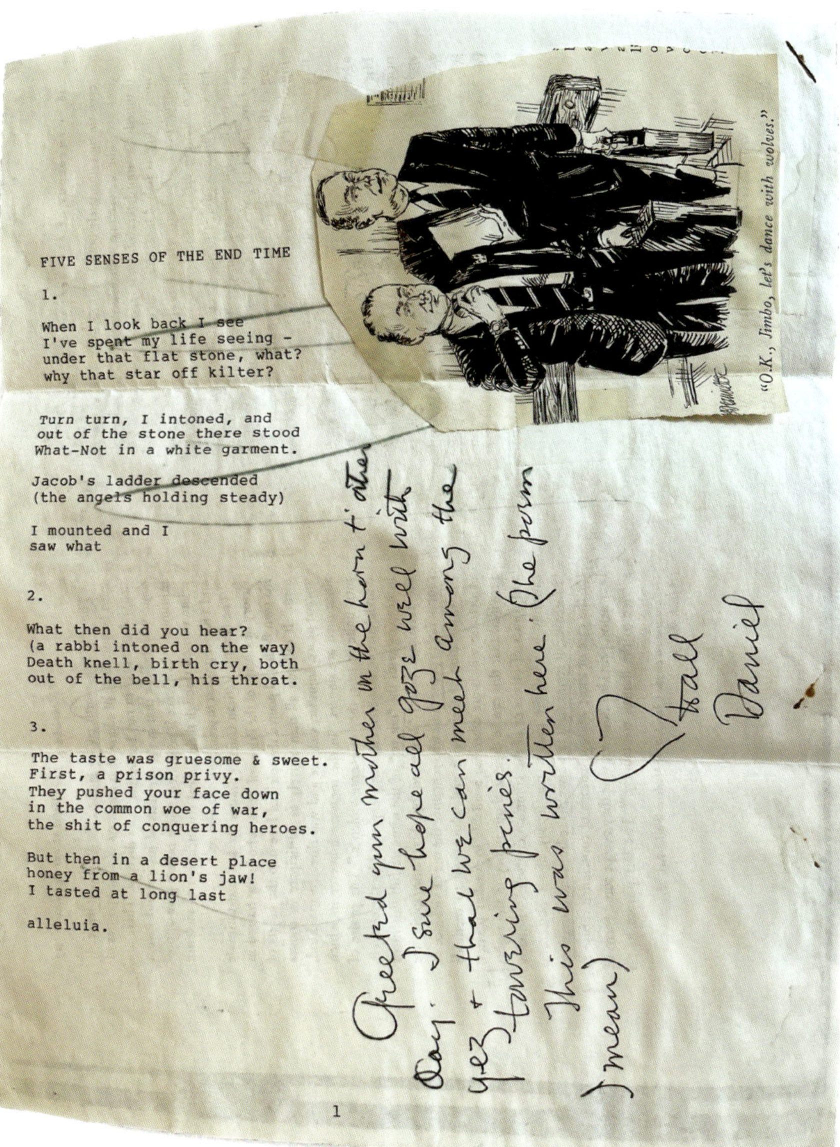

FIVE SENSES OF THE END TIME

1.

When I look back I see
I've spent my life seeing -
under that flat stone, what?
why that star off kilter?

Turn turn, I intoned, and
out of the stone there stood
What-Not in a white garment.

Jacob's ladder descended
(the angels holding steady)

I mounted and I
saw what

2.

What then did you hear?
(a rabbi intoned on the way)
Death knell, birth cry, both
out of the bell, his throat.

3.

The taste was gruesome & sweet.
First, a prison privy.
They pushed your face down
in the common woe of war,
the shit of conquering heroes.

But then in a desert place
honey from a lion's jaw!
I tasted at long last

alleluia.

1

Prison Craft
A bloom of Paint Brush
Plucked unadorned
Paper and tape
Artfully purloined
Pressed with
Books Rocks
A smile
Conspired
Presenteth
Thee
Humbly

June 15 —

Jimbo dear— A prisoner sent this.
I'm going to the Eyeland (Block that is, the 25. We'll have flags + dancers out 4 you — Come soon! And please call when you git north.
I may be on the mainland June 30 for a wedding anniversary
Nice chat with your mother. She sez someone will check on the H_2O.

♥ to all there! Daniel

17 Apr.

Dear brother Jim—

So many thanks for your good letter + the news.
This is to let you know I'm gonna flee New Bedlam in late May for the sea, probably around the 23rd.
Who knows, mebbe you could cut loose for a few days to visit family + such. And I could teach you how to boil water + a soft egg.
Everything's pretty good here. I leave in a week or so for retreat with the C. Worker in Phoenix.
Rob called. He sed how about coughing up that lost wedding license. I sed, I swear Jimbo must have it.

♥ to you + all, Daniel

Dear Jim —

25/3/85

I've tried phoning but no luck, presume you're working most of the day.....
Just a note to say I hope things have settled down, all the sorrow and crowds, since Billl's death, and that you've been able to have a little normalcy and solitude.... I think of you much, knowing how Bill's death afflicted all of us.

I'm wondering also about a few things around the cottage. A young woman wrote me about paining the place, I can't recall if it needs it that badly, also I have no idea of the cost. Could you give a looksee and let me know?

Also we brought up with Ned Hastings the fact that the doctor next door had broken the water and electric lines; I remember that he also broke the phone lines somewhere alng the road next to the white farmhouse (I forget the name). Has anything been done to hasten repair on his part? or should I get to Hastings directly?

Will you be around during the summer?

I'm leaving on Easter Sunday for Cartegena, Colombia, for 3 months, back the end of June; but then I begin 2 weeks teaching in N. Orleans. But after that it wd. be great to cometo the island. Will you be there this summer?

Please be well, and my affectionate best to you and family,

Dan Berrigan

late evenings best for calling.

July 31, St. Ignatius day

Dear brother Jimbo,

Wotta nie day to sit down & say hello & thanks for the letter & so much more!!!

Yes it was a terrific few days with yall on the Island. And then I went back another week, and your mother was so attentive and everything went well once more. I don't hafta tell her favorite son what a grand lady she is. For the present also having a lonely time of it, trying to figger out the future, cut losses, tack her life into new winds & climes. She'll do fine. I guess I mention things you already know because I sense so strongly her need of support from you, and some attention, as she tries for a new life.

Yes it was a bizzy bizzy week. The po'try reading went just fine, big crowd, and I made friends with the new priest, who seems to me a great improvement on the former incumbant. By the bye (and I guess for the present this is between ourselves) Dr. Claude tol' me that Randall is dickering with her to buy the Breydert house to retire to. I can only wish him ghosts by night & bushels of moped dust by day. It's a foolish move on his part, Claude sez she could scarcely bear the mad roar of the idjits right outside her door.

Claude was finally persuaded by Bryan of Square One, to hold a final show of the Breydert work in the summer St. Andrew's. It was a great success, but sorrowful too, as she packed everything up immediately afterward to take along to Paris. Everything that is, but one mosaic, the Raising of Lazarus, which she wants to give to the Supportive Care hospice where I work. So I'm in process of getting that settled. Meantime, the splendid mosaic graces the cottage. I told Claude this was all quite mysterious, as years ago Katherine loaned me the same mosaic for all of one summer. I remember well how Tony lugged the piece down in their jeep. So it's something of a full circle.

Bob also had a good week in the cottage, and of course your mother and he hit it off wonderfully. He's not been so well of late, but we think we've finally gotten to the root of it all; he had a big polyp removed from the colon two weeks ago; has to go back for more exploratory. But he's already picking up.

I dunno if you want sometime to tool up here for a bit of overnight r&r. There isn't much time left before I depart for N'Ohleens, August 20. I'm going to rent this place out for three months.

It promises to be quite an autumn for us all; what with you intent on Isaiah, & the law'n'order boyos hot on the tails of the eight of usns. Well we'll see; as I allus sez, we're in better hands than their clammys!

See yall the 5th! Dan

1

Dear Jimbo, Monday, 24 June

Absolutely wunnerful to have yours. I'm so delighted that you're settled at last in quarters that befit a towering giant of Yoga!

I wanna help with the Pots & Pans division. Check enclosed.

Of course the Big Bowl of the Pasta Universe is yrs. Difficulty is getting it to you. I could undoubtedly wear it on my pate like the burden of a jungle porter, but prob'ly this wouldn't be well received in ecclesiastical quarters, head or hind.

Any suggestions? There are always things to be carried to the Island (books, pictures etc.) but this all will have to wait on transport. I'd hoped John Dear (who arrives on the island this Friday) would be driving, making a pit stop overnight here. But alas, he's flying Richmond-Westerly-BI, so that out is out.

Do you have wheels? if so, could you come to NY anytime soon, pick up aforementioned Bowl of Love's Labors Lost, together with other chattels?

I expect to come on July 4, after John. By air or by sea, I don't know as yet. I'll phone OUr Lady of Peace to see if Fr. Bob is around. Otherwise I'll fly it.

One feels like mourning for the trees of the island and alas our ~~loved greenery of the cottage, so afflicted~~. It'll be good on the other hand, to see what you propose or've been able to do for replacement - a tough proposition no doubt.

And so many thanks for the attention to the place. We'll hafta celebrate.

The clipping on the Trappist martyrs came my way via Bob Keck. The account of the Xavier party was in the B'more Sun of all places. Everyone seems to echo your sense of the evening.

Please lotsa luv to you, Mamah, Papah, Annie & all friends.

Soon!

Sorry for the patchup. I'm slowly getting this technology-) ...

Daniel

29 Aug.

Dear bro Jimbo,

John Dear + I had an encouraging visit with your mother. She is alert + on her feet + improves day by day. Thank God – a hard surgery and a noble survivor!

I'm keeping the BI cottage unoccupied all of October – and beyond if you so need – for your recuperation.

→ Can you drop me a few lines, hopefully seconding my hope? ←

9 of us were arrested here Nagasaki Day. Court in September. As Chicken Little chirps: "You do what you can!"

Love
Daniel

Dear bro Jimbo – Is it time 2 Start tree planting? Wanna hold a treasure hunt in the cottage? 5 the winner, 500 clams!

"For my part,
I believe that
the vain-glorious and the violent
will not inherit the earth...
In pursuance of that faith
my friends and I
take the hands of the dying
in our hands.
And some of us travel
to the Pentagon
and others live
in the Bowery
and serve there,
and others speak
unpopularly and plainly
of the fate of the unborn
and of convicted criminals.
It is all one."

Daniel Berrigan, S.J.

I should get there Friday 13 October. Mark writes Mev is worse. I'm praying every day. Hard times in Newport-News. Alas. Are you OK? Love, + 4eZ, mamah + papah! Daniel

The Center for Justice of Buffalo
the Buffalo Chapter of Feminists for Life of America and
The Newman Center of the University at Buffalo

are pleased and honored to present

peace activist, philosopher, poet, priest and author
Daniel Berrigan, S.J.

We would like to extend a special thanks
to Msgr. J. Patick Keleher and the Newman Center
at the University at Buffalo for hosting this talk tonight
Thier generous finacial support also made
advertizement on WBFO possible.

We would also like to thank
St. Joseph Cathedral and St. Joseph-University
church for cosponsoring tonights
presentation.

PROGRAM:

MC: Harold N. Harden, Campus Minister

Welcome: Rev. Jacob C. Ledwon
Pastor, St. Joseph-University R.C. Church

Introduction: Mary Stengel

Speaker: Daniel Berrigan, S.J.

Reception: Will follow in the Jane Keeler Room

"The Dream Lives On" mural on the front of the Resource Center for Nonviolence, honoring the Reverend Dr. Martin Luther King, Jr., was conceived and painted by 5th and 6th grade students from Gault Public Elementary School in Santa Cruz, California to mark the King Federal Holiday in January 1987.

Dear Jimbo – It wuz absolutely terrific to have yrs., which I immediately framed + put right next 2 photo of J.P. II, Gandhi, Merton + Reagan. I sure hope the work there is not too awful + that you can get a bit of R+R too. ... My poor brother John is still quite incapacitated, main trouble paralysis of throat + no speech or swallowing... But a good spirit despite all... Hope you hit the Apple soon. ♡ 2 you + family + Mary + Marguerite – Dan

For additional copies:
Resource Center for Nonviolence,
515 Broadway, Santa Cruz, CA 95060
(408) 423-1626.

Thanks for ## also.

New York, N.Y. 1988

USA 22 Connecticut

Jim Reale on the Island.
Block Island
Rhode Island
02807

Dear Jim –
Good times!
I left laundry.
Will you please bring
package to me at
Kirkridge? (left by
Claude, too heavy for me.)
I'll pick it up there.
Called Jerry + Carol.
They send love. Expect

you weekend after
Kirkridge.
Hope party went well.
Time here was wonderful.
♥ to mother + all –
Especially to you!
— Daniel.
FROZE (terrific) apple sauce.
Enjoy!
I borrowed a pair of pants

Dear Jimbo bro, Aug. 6

So many thanks for the taken-on-the-spot candid shot of yrself & bro. You both look, so to speak in the pink. Please have heart & blood pressusre tests taken immediately, do;n't think twice of the expense, send the bill here.... Also will you both please consider cutting down to FOUR session at the trough each day. I have it on the advice of Frank Fortcamp that that's brought himm down in two years, to 250 lbs. Also will you please find out immediately and get a signed affadavit to the effect that theose 2 specimens in the snapshot, are not to be placed on poreine death row? maybe you shouldn't be sleeping so much inthe sun, and shd. get a lawyer immediately, someone who's had experience in saving porkers from the knife. I dunno. But I worry/. Remember Orwell; all pigs are equal, but when aUTUMN comes, suddenly some pigs are more equal than oithers. oink oink.

I spoke to mother R. this am. She's to spend the evening with Jerry & Carol. She sez she hopes you'll have a few days breather onthe island. I'll be there until the 25. Then back to NY where I hope we can reconnoiter before youtake off.

Love to you, ham, pork chops, pickled feet, crackle, bacon, all of you. And to Greg, it'd be real fine if you & bro would stop getting all four trotters in the trough & give Greg a chance. He's looking more & more like the runt, ain't you 2 ashamed????

Daniel

Mark 8:18, 17

Dear Jimbo, 28 Jan.

Yours came today. I think the Bruce/Lynn sojourn is just what the cottage is for. They haven't gotten to me as yet; I think a simple solution would be for you to work out dates with them. The only prospective resident I know of beside yourself is John Dear; I gave you his dates I think; Feb. 23 - March 6.

Looks as though I won't be able to lave my bones in the Fountain Of Youth this winter, perhaps until May, when I could tarry on the Island after the Stringfellow weekend.

The situation of Ned is not immediate danger, only long term, & given the past awful months, no real prospects for return of health, short of the miraculous. I guess you know a 'second team' from Sloan-Kettering has declared the cancer inoperable. I was at Montefiore with him for the second dose of 'new' chimo Friday. If cancer spells quick death, this poison now & then slows the advance of the dark angel - but that's all that can possibly commend it.

Anyway Bob Keck and I have been offered an apartment in San Juan once more, and are going with Ned Feb. 14 for a week. He's delighted with the idea. And to give a notion of his splendiferous good humor, he and I are cooking dinner for the community tonight, with dessert from you-know-what famed concoctors of frozen goodies.

We had a day of retreat today with Kairos, planning events for 50th of Hiroshima. Elmer pretty much led us in and out of Mississippi turns on Mark Twain's raft, a guided tour, replete with flowery rhetoric, of the unknown. I was ast to give a bible reflection and used the enclosed adaptation (forgive me, great ancestor!) as a theme. Afterward they bore me about the neighborhood on their shoulders & declared me an alternate pope. So the ol' ego is snugly in place.

Congrats on the yoga develolpments. Give them also a biblical meditation, so folks don't disappear in their own navels.

P.S. I sent on the B I phone bill, which I paid minus war tax. Did you receive it?

D.

Sorry to be late for your birthday.
Mebbe we can celebrate *again* when I get there –
(you know, the usual, vodka on the house!)
Every year your friendship means more to me.

Every day:
all day,
birth day
!

Daniel

PS Some recent
Stuff 2 while away the
gliding hours . . . .

PRISON, 2,001 (for Philip)

This is dignum et justum, the exact
address of the just.

This fits like a skin a frame
the tegument of noble souls, your soul.

Over hill and dale of nightmare,
for the crowning of saviors –
barbed wire,
miles of it, indicting, arresting the sun,
betraying pure light for a Judas shekel –

woven on hell's loom, bristling with ironies
hell knows nothing of,
it keeps the unjust out (judges,
sheriffs, beware) who throw the just in,

into this thorny nest
where the future broods precious eggs unborn.

O my brother, ten like your soul, only ten,
and the times are redeemed.
You, Susan, Greg, Steven – God keeps count,
wills the total –

like a priest's cup passed, full, unfailing,
breathing sacrament.

11 Feb.

Dear Jimbo.
So many thanks for yours!
Yes, I echo all warm sentiments and friendship.
I'll await more definite word on date for Italian
departure. My own sense is June 5 NY–Rome (and train to)
– Parma, then on to Venice; – Rome – NY on 11 June. But we
can adjust. Want you to see Parma, an exquisite more manageable
Firenze.
Phil + Susan you may have heard, each sentenced to one
year for parole violation. Wicked judge Carter laid it on. The
poem is an attempt to cope with pain and loss. Elmer, Frida.
Ian, Bob Keck + I came from NY, people drove all night from all
over. Lets build a stone tower–hermitage – go for it!

Love
Daniel

The Ardagh chalice

The Early Medieval period saw the development of new techniques in metalworking and decoration. The Ardagh Chalice, which dates from the 8th century, is probably the finest object made in Ireland during the first millennium A.D. It was found in a ringfort near Ardagh, Co. Limerick in 1868 where it may have been hidden to protect it from Viking raids or some other serious threat. The bowl, foot and handles are made of silver. A wide variety of techniques were used in the making of the chalice. These include filigree work, complex casting, glassworking, foil stamping and engraving.

Photo © The National Museum of Ireland.

17 Monday, Nov.

Dears,
I found the enclosed in a drawer here, have mailed those
addressed to (I guess) friends in Detroit - a happy
reminder of your time here.
Arrived Friday after touring with Isaiah in NY +
Boston. Isaiah I hope was not entirely displeased. I
think perhaps Bill's comments helped placate the Great Un.
Could, I guess, have mailed this card from Ireland,
but things were hectic with trips Dublin - Belfast - Galway,
poetry reading + radio + meetings with old friends.
The Island is rocking with the First Warden McGovern +
2 cronies indicted for rape, McG. dethroned by Kim
Gaffett in a hasty write-in. Her father, it will be remem-
bered, slapped up (sic) the cottage, a job so nefariously
deficient we refused to pay the last installment. Kim is a
different sort, printer + school bus driver.
News from Hastings on the estate losses truly awful. I
wonder what we're 2 do when the music stops?
Jim Reale leaves for India in early December to seek
I guess the buddha's tooth.
The newly planted trees, severely fenced from deer
depradations, survived the first noreaster. Gifts of Jim
R., Jim Wallis + John Dear.
The Kellerman deck holds firm. Gratias.
I go in late November to Birmingham for retreat with
Douglasses + friends. Bizzy Dizzy.
Met, for first time, nephew of Bill S. at a gathering in
Boston. He averred that on my demise the cottage is to pass to
the Audubon Society. That news + Ben + Jerry largesse, makes
me want 2 linger longer.
We have John Dear with us in NY, also Steve Kelly,
underground, refusing terms of parole. 8 marshalls shoved one →

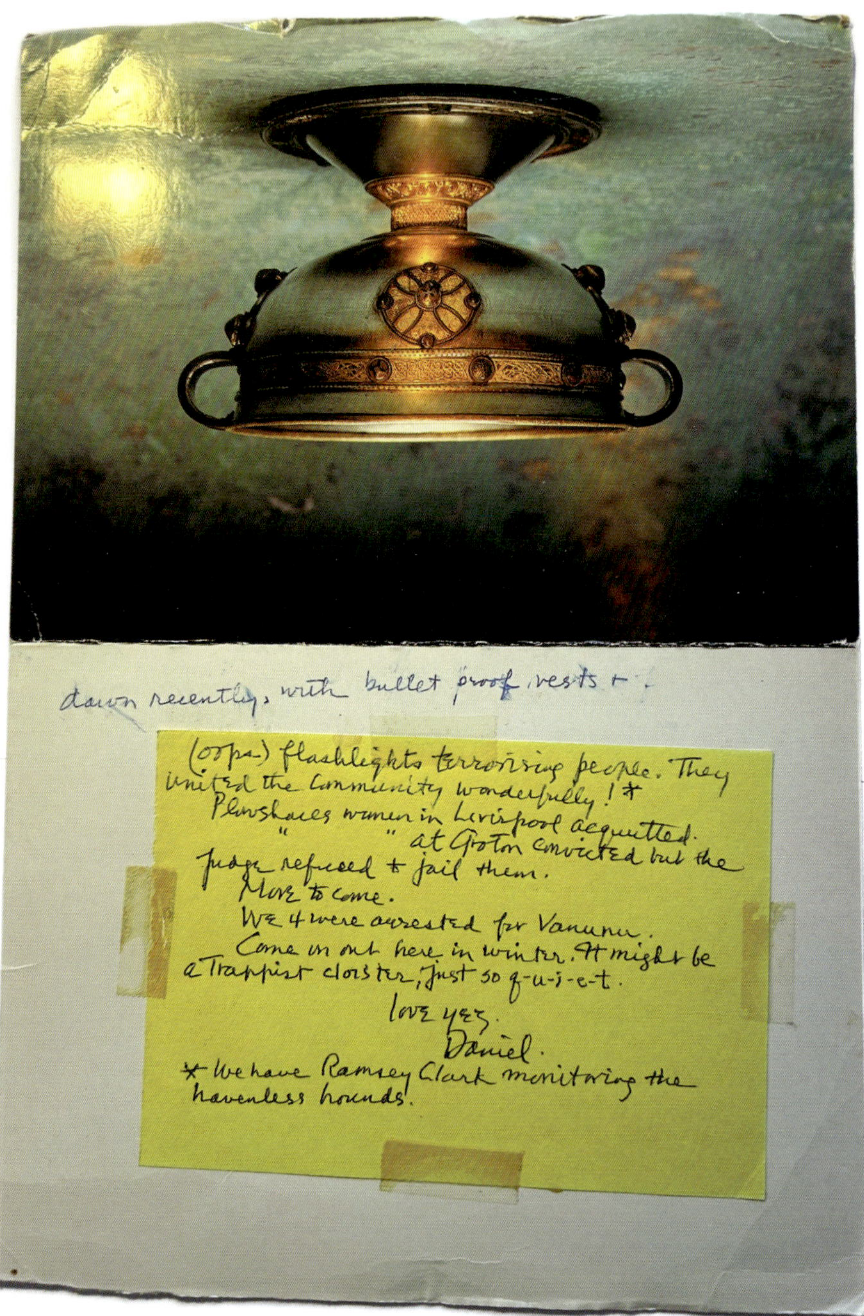

down recently, with bullet proof vests + .

(oops.) flashlights terrorising people. They
united the community wonderfully! *
Plowshares women in Liverpool acquitted.
" " at Groton convicted but the
judge refused to jail them.
More to come.
We 4 were arrested for Vanunu.
Come on out here in winter. It might be
a Trappist cloister, just so q-u-i-e-t.
love yez.
Daniel.
* We have Ramsey Clark monitoring the
haverless hounds.

Dec. 8. —— 1980
Dears, I feel I've been ignoring you, all unwitting: just seems as though things here never stop (where do they?)
the B. Island thing was cut short doo 2 a series of teknikle catastrophes. It was colder'n hell's walk in freezer + the furnace gave out. I was willing 2 be minor-league heroic until 1 day. Sittin' in the sun + pickin' my nose. I heerd waters of Siloe under me. Examination revealed (you gessed) a spraying pipe. No plumber. Bill away 4 the day. Finly called Mr. Larson who responded, w- flashlight pointed out turn off. I crawled in, did it, but the episode sorta broke the honeymoon. Home herein N.Y where so 2 speak everything's normal.
Well. Fr. Joe McVeigh (over) did 3 day fast draped in blanket, night + day, front of U.N. Then a day at British consulate. Then a Sister (p.2) took over + did 2 days of same. There are these great things happening as the

Daniel Berrigan to Dears, December 9, 1980. Jerome C. Berrigan papers, box 5, folder 19.

Special Collections and Archives, DePaul University Library, Chicago, IL.

Dears, (Thursday, Sept. 23) 1982
As will by these presents be apparent, I made it out here. What is not so easily conveyed, is the autumn beauty of the island. Today I surprised five cormorants on the rocks, last night we saw four deer calmly gazing & grazing on the pro-petty. Golden rod and rose hips & queen anne's lace, at least these.
Two days rain, then today everything busted out jus like Oklahoma.
Bill seems pretty good, we haven't had a chance for deep palaver yet. Bill Kellerman was here after the Dean Hammer wedding, left on early ferry today.
I must also report a migrating turtle today, and last night also, a genuwine Block Island vole on the path. I jes about missed the lil tad with my boot. They are only found here, as Anthony was happy to tell, and rarely seen even on the island.
The big news, and sad but for circumstances, is that Aldo the baker died Monday and was buried in Providence today. It was a mercy. Only two weeks ago, Dan, Bill and I had pizza there and Aldo sat down to join us, speaking with great difficulty, thought it was clear he understood us. The family have closed shop; by all accounts it is dubious whether they'll return in the spring.
A strange saga opened up before I left America. It appears that a married priest whom I knew for years and helped as needed, was picked up in O klahoma in possession of a stolen car. He was extradited and brought east to Jersey for trial. Meantime, Elaine had split & gone to Florida to live with family. She called in a panic to give the news. I got busy, feeling like the original Elmer Glue. Some priests at Seton Hall hleped, we're presently raising his bail. This couple is the origin of the concept of 'born loser'-which I guess is their credential....anyway it was heartening to find Christians among the clergy; they got right on the stick.
As I'll be at Seton Hall in early Oct., I'll see my friend, in or out.
Ned Murphy had a fine evening Monday, a benefit for his house, at Ramsey Clark's office. Jay Dudgeon sang and I yapped briefly. Waitll you see the table Jay made for the apahtment!
I guess that does it for the nonce. Except many friends are sick & yer thought & prayer solicited.

Daniel Berrigan to Dears, September 23, 1982. Jerome C. Berrigan papers, box 6, folder 2. Special Collections and Archives, DePaul University Library, Chicago, IL.

Friday - 16 May /1980

Dears,
You can read this front or back, about = sense. The backis sanscrit and buddhist notes by=Joe Roccosalvo, this side is me. Im writing this on the porch in crisp blue noon, that dream weather I cant bottul & send you but iwsh I could...Got in yere last night about 5. Frederick was at the air port, we were a half hour late taking off from Westerly, and an hour late arriving there by chouchou from NY. Bill someone the pilot has an elegant lil new plane where you sit chop to shop, it's all velvet plastic tubing, like the inside of a flying casket.
Bill S. is fine, but he dont care much about eating alone, so the food last night was minimal.(Ill fix all that.) There was water trubbel and heat trubbel and the usual folderol on 1st. night here. Quite hilarious. The fun is to start Sunday with the Solemn High Ashes, we're to dispose of Anthony right under the flag pole about 2 PM, then a great rusty anchor will mark the spot. I jes hope Billy doesnt dig him up some full moon. Its to be quite a crowded assembly, what with folk from the mainland and so on, a short prayer service, then much munching and mingling. Ill be glad when its all over! Bill's sent a sort of solemn starched-front notice to about 30 people.
Frederick is in solitary spelndor at the island house, the bride is all set to arrive here sometime in May. I lose the sequence in these uxorious intercontinental events; but itappears there is yet another operation to be done on F., after which he will live one hundred years without stopping. He's taking me shopping for essentials today, and purportedly to mail this as well; luckily there are only rabbits and pheasants making for town these days, so this is not necessarily a farewell note.
→ By the way, the Mayers are going west this summer, so your two weeks here are assured!!! ←
The Franklin stove is in but not of. That is to say, there are various connections still disconnected. But it does make a handsome squat conversation piece, and since no heat issues, one can elevate nether limbs and thus avoid embolisms. Also geraniums could be planted in various mysterious orifices. We'll see, being mothers of invention.
I trust the Bmore days were nice and easy.
Had a long newsy letter from Jim Tyler, it appears John Deedy wants to stop by you. That should be nice.
I'm reading Faulkner's letters. Wuz a bit dismayed to read he went on treks for state dept, once he got famous. O well. Im here till Wednesday (21 May)

♡ Daniel

Daniel Berrigan to Dears, May 16, 1980. Jerome C. Berrigan papers, box 5, folder 19. Special Collections and Archives, DePaul University Library, Chicago, IL.

1980
11 July. Dears; I enclose a photo of meself/wandering the fields here, decked out by nature's largesse, thinking also how nice it's going to be when you arrive. Yestiddy stopped to see Frederick and meet for first time, the fabled Claude. She turned out to be a quite nice, warm hearted but cool plated pro. She gave us a rundown on Freedrick's condition which seems quite unexpectedly serious; now it devolpps they have discovered an aneurism in the groin, just where one artery branches out into the 2 chief ones of the legs. Much doubt that a plastic bypass could be arranged, given his age and condition. So she said,'we must live from day to day'.. He goes into hospital/again for those endless tests which are the bane of so many.. They are going to come for dinner Monday, and I'll go there for a eucharist later in the week. They depart for France on 6 August, depending of course on his condtion.
I'm unsure of how much of all this F. knows.
The place here is in top condition. The Franklin stove is installed and hums away, I tried it out last night, as it was quite cool. The exterior of the house is painted, same blue and white. Only one cracked board remains in the deck. Both screen doors repaired and functioning. All this and more,careof Bill Kellerman, my young minister friend and former Union student, who was visiting and worked away like a benign demon. (He wouldn't take a $ for his splendid work.)
At the Great House on the Hill, things are also being torn apart and put together. There is a stone mason working on the exterior study walls; he will have it so cunningly insulated that this winter, no rude weather will prevail, no furnace need be invoked. Or so one is told. There are also plans for an enclosed garage, new windows in study and bedroom (more light and heat) etc etc.
Well the burthen of all this as they say, beyond mere warm gossip, is to assure you the goose hangs high & yr. welcome awaits. There will be no laborious tasks in the enclosed garden or dwelling, only muted revels by night and ambrosia and nectar by day. You'll see!
The swimming pool has not been filled. The fry will have to content themselves with the Atlantic Ocean. An austere life, but bracing.
Presently and in prospect, I am doing, to put matters shortly, nothing. I look out on the lilies of the fields and the bluefish of the sea, and their message is one of non urgency and above all else, non efficiency. Thus they correspond to my innate ideas. Let others dig and beg and spin. I shall be the son of the lotus and the friend of the unicorn. ♡
Enough balderdash. Eden awaits. Come precipitously.
Daniel

PS Mindful and prayerful about folk at pentagon and hopeful all is well.
Did I mention Tony Walsh is at 98 St., dwelling in 11-L for this week? We had 3 good days together

Daniel Berrigan to Dears, July 11, 1980. Jerome C. Berrigan papers, box 5, folder 19. Special Collections and Archives, DePaul University Library, Chicago, IL.

Dears — First day —

I think I'd better stick 2 home port in August. The campaign here at Riverside is going well, I've 2 court dates this month (who knows what?) before leaving 4 Berea. Also you already are thrice loaded with domestic talent - beginning with yourselves!

The B. Island situation is not encouraging. Poor John literally at sea in the big house. And more 'development' a looming threat. Sometimes I think we shd. just take the holy ashes up, sprinkle them at sea, & just leave the place 2 the wreckers + dollars. O well!

The card is by a friend, who works with me with AIDS ill.

Never the less! blessed new year Daniel

Daniel Berrigan to Dears, August 31, 1981. Jerome C. Berrigan papers, box 6, folder 1. Special Collections and Archives, DePaul University Library, Chicago, IL.

Wed. — 15 Sept '82

Dears · I hope you enjoy this 'effusio' which kept me out of the B.I pubs for a wk. or so.

I'm desolate about John Leary's death. He was a soul of quality as to be Dorothy Day's son. What are we do do with these young people jogging their hearts to a stop!? Please send the 2 sheets on him to Phil + Liz?

Keck returned aglow + now coping with new teaching and reentry into Macadamville. You all did good things!

The C. Worker article on Jerry + academe has had good words around. Someone also sent me Philly paper + article on Allenwood which I must still get to. Photo of Jerry stunning.

I'm going to N. London trial Monday, benefit for Ned's house at Ramsey's office in P.M., then off to B. Island for another week. Bill was in N. Orleans most of my time there. We had almost no serious talk about his eyes + future.

FINALLY Pat O'Brien got a call through. NO CANCER! He'll come to mainland, meet me in Dublin airport & we'll go to Clare together. Great relief!

Much ♡ Daniel

P.M., P.S. Hope you like Rome.

10 Feb. '97

Dears, and then some!
I'm here just short of durance vile, shipped off by the community after claim was laid to the frame by a pestilential incursion of something akin to flu - and thriving in bones & marrow since around thanksgiving! Tested for every ill native to our kind, nothing conventional, not a blip. So I learn patience, but barely.

OiMoi. Besides a dirge, this goes to say I hope the Michigan winter is being merciful. I was forced by medicos & friends to cancel the Grand Rapids stint; probably sensibly. But it wasn't easy, I thought of (and invoked) Bill & his courage & creeping incapacities.

Well I discovered on the shelf here # 2 of the Works In Progress, and the purely delighteful essays therein of Anthony. Undoubtedly your eyes' gimlet has already found these. But I wanted to register my own surprise, even wonderment. I hadn't known for instance, that Anthony like Bill, had been afflicted with a military stint. Or that what he saw in postwar Japan turned him around like a dervish, or upside down like Peter the Apostle on the cross.*

Please, love to you all. And so many thanks for the magazine, sprightly, instructive, alive.

Dan Berrigan

*P.S.
I'll bring #2 to NY with me, just in case you want to see it—

PPS
I'm not to be thought responsible for the sentiments on back of the card. Oi-moi once more!

Wednesday - 1 Sept 1982

Dears - Hyar I am settin' in the
sun + thinking of yez, the good times
Even though brief, the departure + time
since. It's been good, the usual, a stop-
ping or at least slowing of clocks, time with
Dan, good cooking, walkin + wadin. (No
swimming, the polar bears are coming closer!)

There's talk of a big storm brewing and
it seems right for once, uneasy winds and
clouds rocking the sun. We'll batten down +
see where it goes. Bill + Dan leave for N'Oleans
Sunday, so I'll be in command of the fort until
Thursday. That'll mean real solitude!

Bill seems in fine fettle, a different man
than before Dan W. arrived on the scene. And
I s'pose you noticed the cannily improved be-
havior of the canine populace?

Anyway. Just a greeting. Hope new
works and classes are starting well. Love to
all at home —

Daniel.

Daniel Berrigan to Dears, September 1, 1982. Jerome C. Berrigan papers, box 6, folder 2. Special Collections and Archives, DePaul University Library, Chicago, IL.

SEEKING

What I didn't seek, came
jangling, an exposed wire, a nerve.
High voltage. Danger. The famous & rich.

Then in great numbers and days, the lucky -
untouched by the leprous hand, Success
that fits shrouds with pockets,
turns Croesus, evasive and average
head to sole, to deaf and dumb gold.

What I sought didn't arrive at first.
I sat for hours, years, in the buddha's palm,
I paced here to horizon
like a psalmist
halfway through a dirge
or a halfhearted alleluia
(God the reluctant prompter)

the train I ticketed,
irretrievable, over the hill, no angel
to speak of.

Until.

Jim-
Wanted to get a card but no go.
So hope the 'pome' suffices, to say thank you
with all my
Daniel

12

THE POEM

concerns a speech that was never given -
joy overtook us. My brother home from prison.
The prose lies there on paper, papery
as lips of the dead. Unheeded.
We needed joy -
O it was granted
joy beyond those words or these - one another.

My words were like eyes, redundant
closed eyes of the dead.
Not for nothing to see,
for everything. Closed against partial sight,
partial world, apportioned seas, approximations
(a bush afire, dew on a fleece, virgins and old women
heavy with hope's children.)

Who needs words?
partial, ourselves in here, in now
part captivated, strangers seeking the right way
from strangers; if lucky, honest strangers,
their 'I'm not sure' the surest signpost
toward love's intersecting
darkness and truth.

(for Philip on his birthday, 10/5/'94)

Jim; fondly, gratefully.
Daniel

TWO WEEKS ON AN ISLAND IN MID-JANUARY WILL DO THIS TO YOU

Here, time is landlocked. Sea
locks it in. Sun, moon, storm,
nothing lasts. 'Nothing should!'
they say in the city,
whose clocks
run fast, run past, like people.

Yesterday, snow owned the yard
like a pall slowly drawn
over a dead face. Imagine,
you saw the snow ever so slowly
draw breath an inch or two
above the face, you were so close
to what just went. You hardly breathe.

The wall stonewalls; big stones,
each a god, the same
back of head, facing
(if so a face), away.

Today, a thaw,
the snow creeps close, curved, cold
as a serpent's lip, for survival.
A thin white line,
then a dark line; impressionists
caught it with careless care, once for all.

The shadow of stone owns
like God, all that barely
makes it this far.

Out at sea, waves a league long
arrive from Portugal, die
like near-heroes, spectacularly ashore.
They resemble the pharoah's
chariots, horses and men
tumbling down, scripture's
expendable, watery warriors.

Another then another, tries and dies.
Obsessed, you say?
Give them credit – that will of theirs
to march straight up the cliff
and return you, every one of you –

back, pharoah barked,
where you belong.

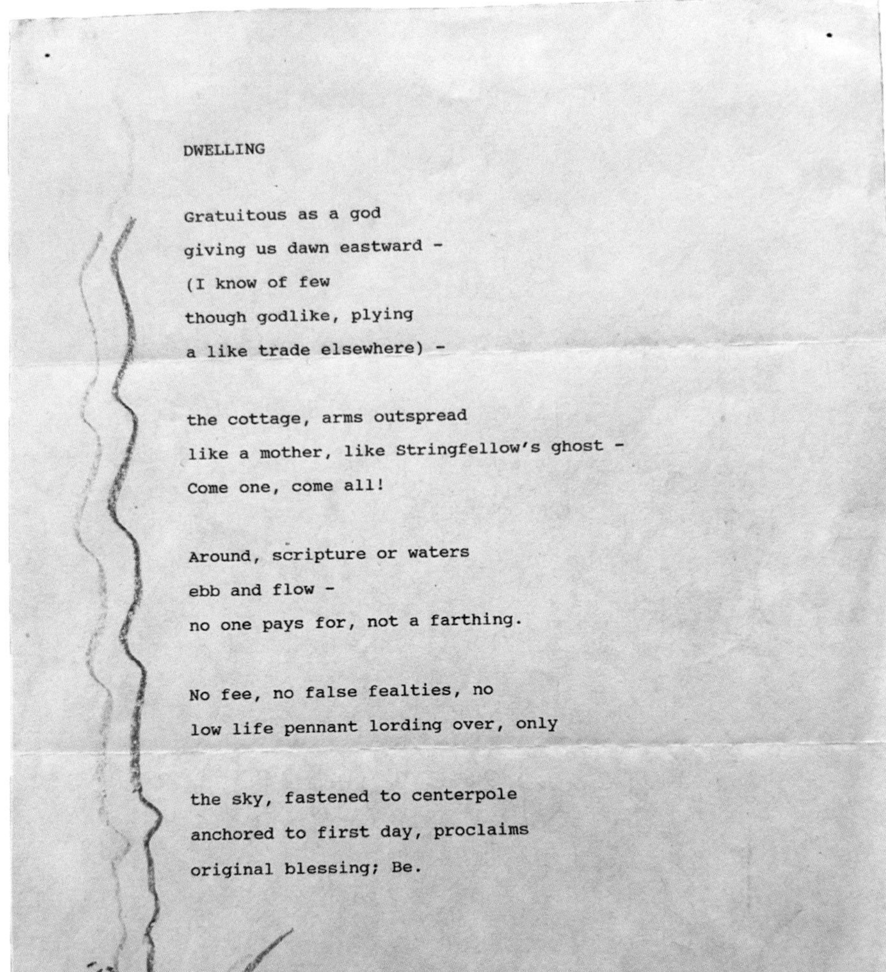

DWELLING

Gratuitous as a god
giving us dawn eastward -
(I know of few
though godlike, plying
a like trade elsewhere) -

the cottage, arms outspread
like a mother, like Stringfellow's ghost -
Come one, come all!

Around, scripture or waters
ebb and flow -
no one pays for, not a farthing.

No fee, no false fealties, no
low life pennant lording over, only

the sky, fastened to centerpole
anchored to first day, proclaims
original blessing; Be.

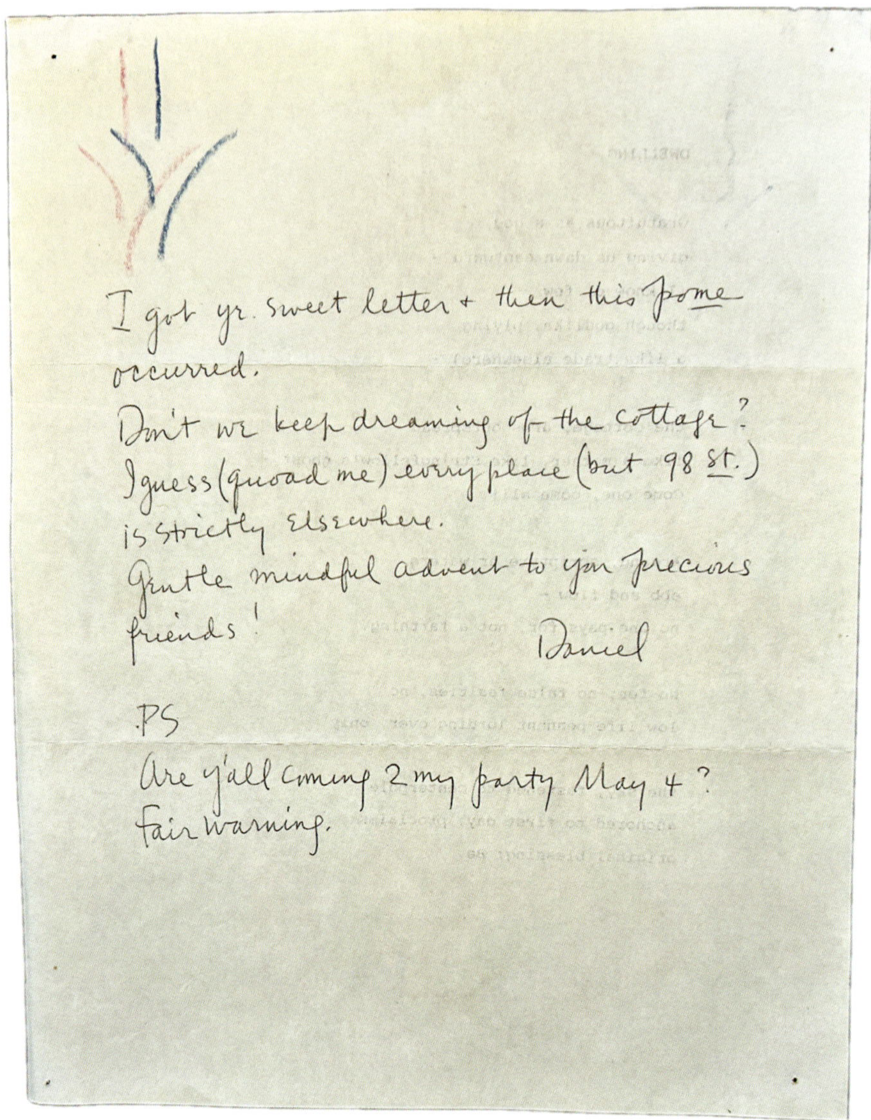

I got yr. sweet letter + then this pome occurred.
Don't we keep dreaming of the cottage?
I guess (quoad me) every place (but 98 St.) is strictly Elsewhere.
Gentle mindful advent to you precious friends!

Daniel

PS
Are y'all coming 2 my party May 4?
Fair warning.

AFTER

When the towers fell
a conundrum;

Shall these from eternity
inherit the earth,
all debts amortised?

Gravity was ungracious,
a lateral blow
abetted, made an end.

They fell like Lucifer,
star of morning, our star
attraction, our access.

Nonetheless, a conundrum;
Did God approve, did they prosper us?

The towers fell, money
amortised in pockets
emptied, once for all.

Why did they fall, what law
violated? Did Mammon
mortise the money
that raised them high, Mammon
anchoring the towers in cloud,
highbrow neighbors
of gated heaven and God?

'Fallen, fallen is Babylon the great...
they see the smoke
arise as she burns...'

We made pilgrimage there.
Confusion of tongues.

Some cried vengeance.
Others paced slow, pondering

- this or that of humans
drawn forth, dismembered -.

a last day; Babylon
remembered.

Hey bro how you bin? I was on
BI during Spring break, visited the
Reales, brought daddy-O communion, had
time with your mother. And fled home with Bob Keck
Easter Sunday. Word was, Dave Toolan was dying after
Brain surgery. (HE'S still in our world, but barely....)
How's by you? Phil has hip replacement 26 April. Love yez—
Dan B.

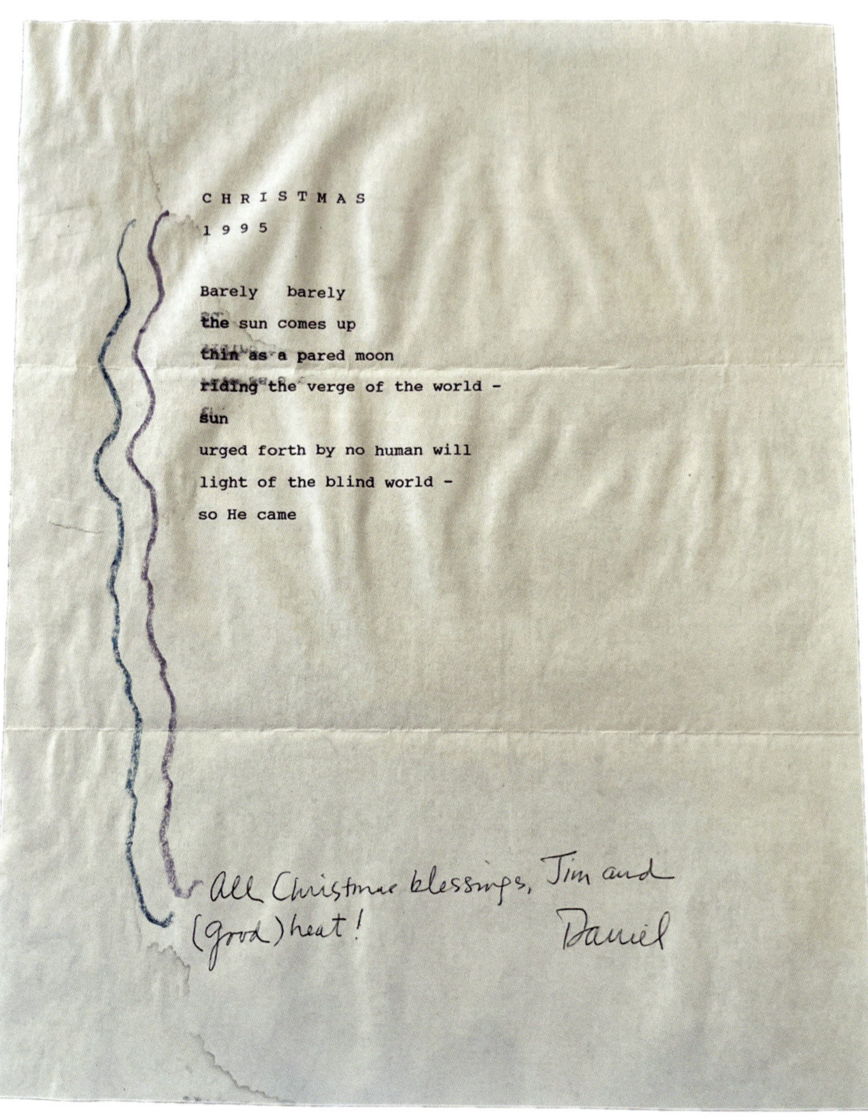

C H R I S T M A S

1 9 9 5

Barely barely
the sun comes up
thin as a pared moon
riding the verge of the world -
sun
urged forth by no human will
light of the blind world -
so He came

All Christmas blessings, Jim and
(good) heat!

Daniel

Dear Ned, December 9, '96

Yours of December 4 received.

Thus I'm appraised of the state of the exchequer; not good.

I've composed a message to guests of the cottage and left it on the premises, inviting contributions. (This is the nearest I'm willing to become, to a dickensian landlord). My brother Jerry and his wife, who visit every summer, have been generous; about 1000 a year. Other gifts have been negligible; not surprising, since the ill and ex-prisoners and such enter the Realm, so to speak, first.

The bigggest summer expense, outside of lawn cutting, phone, power, propane, was the replacement of trees. We have 12 beautiful varied species carefully planted and well protected against deer. These replace the pines destroyed by the onslaught of turpentine beetles, which have devastated the island.

Cost of the above; nearly 700, 300 of which was the gift of Jim Wallis, Jim Reale and John Dear. The rest from me.

Jim W., Scott and Ned have been wonderfully generous, relieving me of large part of the financial burden of the hallowed place. I'm grateful beyond words.

Let's continue in the best Stringfellonian fashion of yinyang, hold on, let go. While the resources last, let the show go on. When the music stops - well, at that point, another decision will be in our hands.

Warmest, awaiting, as 'eschaton',

I wanted you, as an obviously major friend of the cottage, to see this. Poor Ned lost us everything but the flagpole - now he sez he's recovered half a flag. Well well. Hope Advent brings light & warmth to yez!

Love

Daniel.

WEST SIDE JESUIT COMMUNITY
220 West 98th Street
New York, N. Y. 10025

April 3

Dear Ned,

So kind of you to send on latest concerning Bill's will and attendant matters.

As to the cottage, I should clarify matters a bit. According to our Jesuit vows, we have no power of ownership or inheritance. But I did help substantially in the building of same, with understanding of indefinite use. I don't know if this poses a problem with regard to the future. It might be possible to transfer any ownership of the cottage, to my brother and sister-in-law, Dr. and Ms. Jerome Berrigan, 106 Maywood Drive, Syracuse, N.Y. 13205. With the understanding that among ourselves, we will be responsible for maintenance, etc.

There is still the unfortunate matter of Pasternak and the phone, electrical and water lines destroyed by his machinery. I am wondering if these could be pursued; I know many promises had been made during Bill's life, none of which has been honored. And of course the cottage is practically speaking, unusable, as long as such conditions obtain.(A few of the family would hope to use the cottage in late June.)

In any case, I shall be out of the country for three months, in Latin America, returning at the end of June. My brother and family will care for any concerns during that time.

Once more my deep gratitude for your kindness and friendship during these difficult times. Bill valued you as one friend in a thousand; and so do I.

Gratefully,

Daniel Berrigan S.J.

SOJOURNERS

P.O. Box 29272 · Washington, DC 20017 · (202) 636-3637

April 10, 1986

Daniel Berrigan
Bill Kellermann
Scott Kennedy

Dear Brothers,

Good news! Syracuse has given us a release on Bill's papers. Cornell is really excited and will make arrangement right away to transfer all of Bill's many boxes from Block Island to the Cornell library where they will keep the Berrigan papers company.

There is another matter that we must resolve--Bill's books. John Pfarr is getting a litle anxious about it. He has boxed up all of Bill's books, which has taken a considerable amount of time and expense. He would like to keep the books and promises to make them widely available from his house. He even has discussed a cooperative arrangement with the Block Island Library. The library, as you remember, is saying, in effect, that they would like the books but couldn't keep them all as a collection. And they would probably ship many of them off for re-sale.

Dan suggests we approach Tony Pappas at the Harbor Church to see if he could use a Bill Stringfellow collection. Tony is friend of John Pfarr's. John says that many of the books are in very bad shape, and many others are not very good books. To this point, I've explored no further options and would like your advise.

Finally, on the dates for putting Bill & Anthony's ashes to rest in the pine grove by the cottage...unfortunately, it looks like travel schedules, new babies, and speaking commitments will make it impossible for all four of us to get together either in the spring or the summer. Therefore, I would suggest that we look toward setting some dates in the fall, preferably September or October. Please look at your calendars, and send me <u>all</u> the dates, in that time period, that are possible for you.

We all seem to agree that the service should be simple and small. I'm assuming that it will be the four of us and Mary and Herb from the island. Please send me the names of any other people you think should be invited, remembering that we want to keep it a small group of close friends.

Thanks,

Jim

JW/sp (signed in his absence)

[ca. May 10, 1973]

WILLIAM STRINGFELLOW
COUNSELLOR AT LAW

BLOCK ISLAND
RHODE ISLAND 02807
TELEPHONE 466-5514
AREA CODE 401

Dear Dan

I am forwarding two estimates for Patmos which Lou Gaffett worked out. One is for the Acorn company house, the other is for basically the same plan custom built by Lou, rather than imported. The two proposals are self-explanatory, I think. What is really involved is the reduction of costs by eliminating Acorn, whose prices have gone up over the printed estimates we previously have seen. We had told Lou we wanted to keep within $15,000, and that prompted his custom proposal.

Apart from reducing costs, the relevant additional factor is time. Under the custom proposal Lou would assemble house units here, in his shop (instead of that being done at Acorn) adding he says about a week's time to the construction period. He expresses confidence that the work can be completed in about a month's time, aiming for completion by the end of May. I think it is realistic to expect delays and this and that, so that completion a month later than that might be about right. Anyway, we are ready to execute a contract with Lou for the custom house within a week or so, unless we hear an outcry from you.

Notice that a fireplace, furnace, carpeting, and a kitchen unit are not included in the cost estimates for either of these proposals. We are trying to get some data on a single kitchen unit, containing sink, cabinets, stove, refrig, such as sometimes are seen in efficiency apartments. That would be a helluva lot cheaper than installing cabinets and appliances separately or thru the contractor. Also we are seeking more data on the most efficient furnace. A franklin type fireplace is probably the best bet and can be had for about $250 (brick would likely be three times that). These are additional costs which, however, can be amortized without difficulty. As for furnishings I think we can locate enough and suitable stuff very economically or for free on the island.

I will ask Lou if he can give us a payment schedule related more specifically to dates, but under his present contract proposal the remainder of the $15,000 working figures would be needed only as he commenced work, May 1 or thereabouts, though I am pretty sure we could adjust the payment schedule if a different breakdown were more convenient.

~~XXXXXXXXXXXXXXXXXXXXXXXXXX~~ I talked with Ned Hastings, our lawyer, just to be sure we are proceeding in an orderly way in the Patmos project and he had some helpful suggestions I wish to discuss with you, so I think I will come to Boston on Sunday, the 25th, then we could grab a half hour to talk at lunch at Lowell Erickson. love

Bill

Daniel and Philip Berrigan Collection, Division of Rare and Manuscript Collections, Cornell University Library

[ca. May 10, 1973]

WILLIAM STRINGFELLOW
COUNSELLOR AT LAW

BLOCK ISLAND
RHODE ISLAND 02807
TELEPHONE 466-5514
AREA CODE 401

Dear Dan

We have been collecting diverse data on Patmos, and need some advice as to how to proceed.

The main thing is inflation. Costs have increased about 30-40% over the 1969 figures from Berger you saw when you were here. I have obtained a current Berger price list which is enclosed, with their latest catalog. In the case of Berger cottages, you must keep in mind the necessity to contract separately for a foundation (add up to $2000), and the result is an erected shell, for which finishing costs would add (bathroom/insulation/heating/ wiring/ plumbing/kitchen facilities) perhaps as much as $4000 more. Here, again a separate contractor would be required. Thus the actual basic cost, without frills or conveniences (like a fireplace) for a Berger cottage would be something like the following:

speptic tank & well connection & wiring underground	2000
foundation/ bulldozer	2000
erected shell	4500
rough finishing	4000
transport/contingency/furnishings/ taxes	1500
	14000

I have also talked with Lou Gaffett (a good guy/local contractor) who is agent for Acorn houses. He has put up three or four on the Island and I have looked at them. They are, material and construction wise, of substantially better quality than Berger. They are of much better design. They have one house which seems very suitable: plans enclosed. They are a bit more expensive than Berger, but you deal with one contractor and the time saving therein is probably very substantial. Lou could get a "rough finish" liveable place up by summer, he thinks. For the plans enclosed the basic cost would be $12000, plus sceptic tank/well/underground wiring/plus transport etc./ for a grand total of something like $15500.

Considering time, quality, design, availability of contrACTOR, etc., I would commend Gaffett's deal, Anthony concurs. But we both wonder if either of these are beyond the means available. If that is so, there are various possibilities (a small mortgage probably could be obtained without too much difficulty) to be discussed. Anyway look over the Acorn, as well as Berger, materials, and give us some reactions. Maybe you could call from a nontapped phone and we could discreetly discuss it. There is some need to get a contract soon if we want a roof up this summer.

Love,

Bill

Daniel and Philip Berrigan Collection, Division of Rare and Manuscript Collections, Cornell University Library

ESCHATON
BLOCK ISLAND, RHODE ISLAND 02807

[ca. Aug. 15, 1975]

V-J Day!
As observed only
in Rhode Island

Dear Dan

Your benevolence causes us to consider a memorial - The denomination of the septic tank, complete with satellites, as "The Daniel Berrigan, S.J. System" or something of the sort. Perchance you will also compose a poem. Anyway, it is in & it does work. But the yard is a mess, greatly aggravating Anthony who even now is out doing some work to rehabilitate the scene (despite a hot afternoon).

Moreover the (huge) Revelation art has just arrived and strangely cheers us. It seems quite correct theologically. It will cause us to rearrange our walls & what hangs from them or on them.

Enclosed a self-explaining letter.

Scott has come & gone. He is a delight. He sorted out all the RW stuff, having quite a good time as he discovered this & that, and it has all been sent to the Syracuse library.

From Syracuse, we presently expect Jerry & Carol. We hope the pool will be clean by their arrival & that the tomatoes are mature.

Daniel and Philip Berrigan Collection, Division of Rare and Manuscript Collections, Cornell University Library

Meanwhile Anthony's mama & friend have also been here, coinciding nicely with various anniversaries — their own birthdays — the Nixon resignation — Hiroshima Day. In the midst of such tumult I wrote the appellate brief for Father Wendt's case.

We saw nor heard anything in the media about your observance of H Day. What happened?

We hope you will come again soon. Remember the fall & the Indian Summer is the best of times here. By then I will, I hope, be finishing <u>Romans 13</u>/<u>Revelation 13</u> and you would prompt my head.

Peace

Bill

Daniel and Philip Berrigan Collection, Division of Rare and Manuscript Collections, Cornell University Library

WILLIAM STRINGFELLOW
COUNSELLOR AT LAW

BLOCK ISLAND
RHODE ISLAND 02807
TELEPHONE 466-5514
AREA CODE 401

3 April
(2 days after the Feast of Fools)

— name for cottage!

Dear Dan

We have now signed the Patmos contract with Lew Gaffett, paid him the first installment and he has ordered lumber, which should arrive presently.

That is about all we have done because of our sick dog. Marmaduke was returned from a week at the Newport Animal Hospital just a week ago. Despite some terrible wounds, for a few days he perked up and even, tentatively, walked a little. Then Sunday his temperature increased sharply and he seemed to be failing. It appears that there is serious internal damage, as we had been warned by the vets, and now his condition is again grave. The vet will come tomorrow to, most likely, return him to the hospital for surgery. Our anxiety is all the more because what internal problems there may be are still unknown and he is not robust enough to suffer much more. It was thought earlier that he had pancreas damage that would render him diabetic and in need of some days in the hospital & then briefly here he had to be given insulin. That condition, which we considered too ironic to contemplate, seems to have abated, however.

The ironic, grotesquely ironic, element in the whole incident is nevertheless still present. It seems certain that of the two dogs involved in the violence against Marmaduke that the chief aggressor is the very dog who impregnated Polly! And his attack on Marm was mainly in the lower abdomen & genitals & in the region of his tail (which was nearly severed.) It's just too much, too bizarre.

Well, we try to care for the dog, and hope for the best.

Mel has perhaps told you that I expect to be in the city April 11th. And we look forward to your visit in Holy Week, when you will be able to school a pile of lumber out toward the cliffs.

Love,

Bill

went to [illegible] the Met Museum
[illegible] in Central Pk. He is
physically feeble, but alert &
cheerful as ever, a Joy.
On that day Dudgeon arrived
with fine oak table for the kitchen
+ tools, + materials put the
kitchen floor in shape! All
sorts a progress impending!
Love
D.

Kellerman also put asbestos
sheets around the stove on the 2 corner
walls. And the mason had to tear
out a new higher vent in the chimney
for the stovepipe, + fill in the old one
from the tin can fireplace. Quite a
job. wait'll you see!
Bill by the way is fine, no trace of
stroke. I'm going 2 try 2 get him to Dr. Rose.
BR 151 Le Printemps Archimboldo
Mary Donnelly nurse, is backing me. Bill is
running again + first warden.

Daniel Berrigan to Dears, July 11, 1980. Jerome C. Berrigan papers, box 5, folder 19. Special Collections and Archives, DePaul University Library, Chicago, IL.

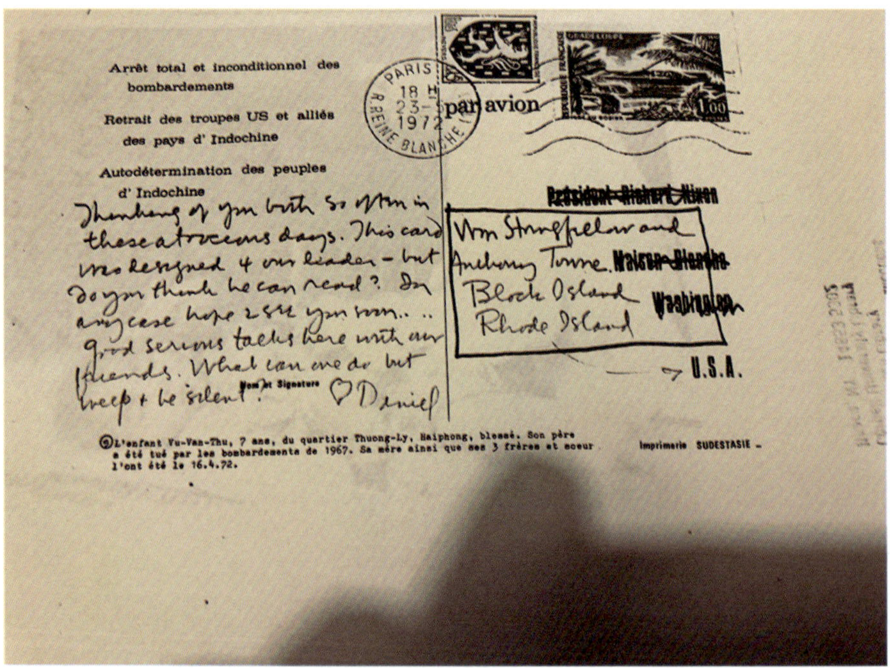

Arrêt total et inconditionnel des bombardements

Retrait des troupes US et alliés des pays d' Indochine

Autodétermination des peuples d' Indochine

Thinking of you both so often in these atrocious days. This card was designed 4 our leader – but do you think he can read? In any case hope 2 see you soon.. .. good serious talks here with our friends. What can one do but weep + be silent? Nom et Signature ♡ Daniel

PARIS 18 H 23-5 1972 R. REINE BLANCHE

par avion

~~Président Richard Nixon~~
Wm Stringfellow and
Anthony Towne. ~~Maison Blanche~~
Block Island ~~Washington~~
Rhode Island
U.S.A.

L'enfant Vu-Van-Thu, 7 ans, du quartier Thuong-Ly, Haiphong, blessé. Son père a été tué par les bombardements de 1967. Sa mère ainsi que ses 3 frères et soeur l'ont été le 16.4.72.

Imprimerie SUDESTASIE –

THE TABLE AT ESCHATON

by Nancy Walker Greenaway

Wooden rectangle snugs up to picture window,
framing anchor, flagpole,
lawn rolling toward village, harbor, sea . . .

Around the table gather people of conscience,
friends of faith, friends for life.

Served here:
readings from the Book of Common Prayer,
obituaries from the New York Times.
curses about treatment of the poor,
support for women seeking priesthood,
strategies for creating an underground seminary
poetry poking fun at claims that God is dead.
scenes from travels with a circus,
life stories about lawyering in Harlem,
encouragement to those devoted to community,
nourishment for those committed to peace,
liquid spirits and laughter.

Meals, ever memorable, begin and end with grace.

Eschaton: "... the end of the world coinciding with the beginning of the world as the Kingdom of God ... eschaton means hope." Name of the Block Island home of William Stringfellow and Anthony Towne where Jesuit priest Daniel Berrigan sought sanctuary after being sentenced to prison for anti–Vietnam War actions.

Epilogue
by Jim Reale

Dear Dan,

Sorry not to have written since your death eight years ago. I've thought of you often but it's not the same as a letter. Lots to catch up on.

Mama

My mother died three years ago. She started her own business, Block Island Realty. Lyn, you may recall, had Alzheimer's disease. All her kids were in the room either physically present or through FaceTime when she drew her last breath. The nurses and certified nurse assistants came in prior to and after her passing to say goodbye, kissing her, telling her stories, openly weeping with their heads resting against her cheek. In all my ten years of hospice nursing, I have never seen such a display of love and affection for a patient. Holding her hands, I prayed the Our Father aloud just moments after her death. It seemed like the right thing to do. Addressing the One who created her.

I was rereading the letters you wrote me over the years. They are treasures and bring you back to mind with lightning speed. You often signed off with "Love to Mama and Papa." One letter in particular stands out. "Dear Jimbo, So great hearing from you. I wrote your mother 2 say thank you for her wunnerful bust at the Air Force [base]. Wotta lady!"

I recall she was at a demonstration that day with Jackie Allen and others from the Hartford Catholic Worker. When it was time to "step over the line," I imagine she leaped! It wasn't the first time she said no to war.

During the early '70s my parents sat us down at the dining room table. It wasn't dinnertime. The Vietnam War was raging and scores of young men were returning home in coffins with flags hiding the sin of war. My mother and father (who was a WWII veteran), declared in no uncertain terms that if any of their sons were drafted, we were on a one-way flight to Canada. Maybe that's where I got my first inkling to follow conscience before country.

Any sightings of Mama in your neck of the Heavens?

Islanders

Barbara and I visited Block Island several months ago and stayed with John and Joanne Warfel. Joanne, who taught English as a Second Language at the school and was a key administrator at the Medical Center, has retired. John also retired from teaching shop class and is now championing renewable energy, has shown his pottery at the Jessie Edwards and Spring Street galleries, and continues to make embellishments on their home. It's a little piece of paradise tucked away on the West Side. We reminisced about our dinners together with you at your cottage and the one-of-a-kind wood stove John designed and loaned us for the many years of cold winters. Their commitment to the BI community is decades long.

I had lunch with Nancy and Malcolm Greenaway. Malcolm continues to capture island-born photographs with greater insight and artistry than ever before. Because there's a shortage of workers here, he is framing all his art himself. He turned eighty though doesn't look a day over sixty-five. Nancy continues to be one of the smartest whips on earth. She gave a poetry reading last week and has published a book of poetry with artwork by Josie Merck. Nancy remains poised, graceful, articulate, and deeply caring. She also retired from the Medical Center, which she germinated from seed and directed with others. They have been married fifty-plus years.

Jiffy Blansfield built her own home in Ebbetts Hollow. With her attention to detail, light, view, and economy of space, she leaves Frank Lloyd Wright in the dust. She has a room dedicated to study in her areas of interest, natural healing and spirituality, among other things. She started a business managing rental homes and is busier than the bees collecting honey for Block Island honey jars. She is clear and strong, savvy and soft. I worry about her son Aidan, who signed a second hitch with the Marines. I am his godfather, yet I couldn't find the words to persuade him otherwise. He cannot see the gifts he has to offer the world when he starts taking orders from the authority within. If you have any sway, please help bring him home safely. Body, mind, intact.

Kim Gaffett, to my mind, is the unsung heroine of the island. It's as if she leads a movement to better the island with quietude and humility, unprompted by fanfare or reward. She has paused on holding public office after decades of thankless work, though continues to perform the Works of Community: working for the Oceanview Foundation, banding birds to track migration, securing fiber optic broadband, and whatever else it takes to battle the winds and waves that erode the island's greatest asset: the people who call it home 24/7, 365. Who raise their children on this tethered porkchop. Who count the living on Groundhog Day. Who bear the next generation and bury those whose number is called to be next.

Annie Hall, my sister (who never kissed Woody Allen, thankfully), in past years has hosted the annual Easter egg hunt with all the island kids invited. She has been on the school committee for a generation and then some, supporting proposals that have given the kids an education and activities exceeding most schools. Annie and Glen's oldest son Jake and his beloved Dee wed in October. It was an island wedding with over three hundred attending. John Grant, a ship's captain and lobsterman, presided over the day for the newlyweds. Best wedding ever.

Mary Donnelly died. She entered the "cloud of witnesses" without even having to show her ID. Have you bumped into her? It's as if in losing her, the island has lost a gargantuan piece of its soul. She was the Mother Teresa of Block Island, except MT didn't have seven kids to raise at the same time while performing the Works of Mercy, Charity, etc.! She was ever so faithful attending the weekly peace vigil downtown. Remember when Mary and Margarite would have us over for dinner, and they would make that shrimp vegetable stir-fry thing? Oh, lots of shrimp, wine, and always a dessert.

I hope I can maintain a friendship with Margarite. I guess I just have to reach out.

Please keep the islanders in your prayers.

You're a Movie Star

We finished the documentary *The Berrigans: Devout and Dangerous*. It took nearly seven years from start to first screening. Well worth it. Sue Hagedorn, with my brothers Rob and Willie, as well as Rick Dresser, myself, and a whole lot more people chiseled the story of you, Phil, and Liz, dedicating your lives to peace, telling of Jesus as the Prince of Peace, architect of nonviolence, quintessential activist.

The film has won several awards in festivals and the audiences are beside themselves with gratitude for the sacrifices made in the name of peace. It will be an educating and organizing tool of nonviolence for years to come.

You're Being Collected

Friends dear to you, Anna Brown, Dan Cosacchi, Colleen Dulle, Eric Martin, Terry Moran, and Bill Wylie-Kellermann, have founded The Daniel Berrigan Collective, promoting contemplation, community, and resistance. It was created to promote the person, thought, and legacy of you, using a variety of media, including writing, art, music, poetry, celebrations, and social media. These fine people convey your writing, spirit, and essence in a way that holds true to your life as witness, sacrifice, sacrament, and friend.

Pray their faith illuminates the hearts and minds of all they encounter.

World News with Commentary

On the world stage, things are worse than ever. Climate change is transforming everything, except the policies of politicians. They are owned by the corporations who profit from no change. Those who don't want to upset the applecart of Wall Street. They are essentially slaves to their corporate lobbyists, except they get to live like their masters.

Phoenix, Arizona, set a record of thirty-one consecutive days of 110-degree heat. Hurricane Helene devasted the South with well over two hundred twenty-nine deaths.

Pray we understand our peril and change our ways before it's too late.

Putin invaded Ukraine. He has threatened going nuclear on several occasions. Perhaps his greatest concern is not to be seen as a loser. Thomas Merton's unmasking declaration in his essay, *The Root of War Is Fear,* comes to mind. Some of the Russian men have fled to avoid conscription. Well done, gentlemen, conscience over country. President Zelenskyy has led his people with determination and courage. He has traveled the world pleading for assistance from other countries, winning hearts and minds. The West has sent several billion dollars' worth of weapons to fight the Russian army.

I found myself silently rooting for more support from the West, more money, weapons, fighter jets, tanks to blow the Russian army off the Ukraine map. Then I realized that's exactly what the powers and principalities want. Choose a side. Because if we take sides, the power of death is victorious. Death doesn't care whose side you're on as long as the killing continues. The innocent children, and their mothers and fathers, pay the greatest price for a war they did not ask for.

Pray for all under the threat of war, especially the children.

The top five arms manufacturers in the world, Lockheed Martin, RTX Corporation, Northrop Grumman, Boeing, and General Dynamics are at the trough, snouts buried deep, gorging themselves on the flesh of the innocent. Happier than pigs in what pigs do best after they lift their heads from feeding.

Pray they fall to the ground, see a "light from heaven, brighter than the sun," and convert to the ways of nonviolence.

Humanity First

Thomas Merton plagiarizes the Divine with the following words: "I am on the side of the people who are being burned, bombed, cut to pieces, tortured, held as hostages, gassed, ruined and destroyed. They are the victims of both sides. To take sides with massive power is to take sides against the innocent. The side I take is the side of the people who are sick of war and who want peace, who want to rebuild their lives and their countries and the world."

So I came back to my senses. I side with humanity. I remember God is in all people. Even when I can't recognize God in others, when I am blindsided by my passions, God remains.

God's Nightmare

Dan, your speech in 1973 on the treatment of Palestinians by Israel was prophetic then and doubly prophetic today. Now, I can clearly see how much Merton influenced you. It's worth a reread: "Berrigan 1973 speech." (Does Heaven have Google?)

Here is the softest portion of what you said fifty-two years ago: "I do not wish to begin by "taking sides"; nor indeed to end by "taking sides." I am sick of "sides"; which is to say, I am sick of war; of wars hot and cold; and all their approximations and metaphors and deceits and ideological ruses. I am sick of the betrayal of the mind and the failure of compassion and the neglect of the poor. I am sick of foreign ministers and all their works and pomps. I am sick of torture and secret police and the apparatus of fascists and the rhetoric of leftists. Like Lazarus, staggering from his grave, or the ghost of Trotsky I can only groan: 'We have had enough of that, we have been through all that.'"

As you already know, Dan, the Israeli government has occupied Gaza and the West Bank for decades. The number of Palestinians killed, wounded, or imprisoned during this time period is impossible to calculate. The number of Palestinian homes bulldozed and land seized to benefit Israeli settlers is also impossible to tally. There have been multiple UN resolutions denouncing the occupation of the West Bank and Gaza by Israel, with an overwhelming majority of nations voting to support the right and freedom of Palestinians to live in peace.

Did you get the news in your parts—on October 7, 2023, Hamas entered Israel and massacred twelve hundred people, many who lived peacefully in kibbutzim. They are holding over two hundred hostages, some who have already been released, some who have died in captivity. Wicked.

The Israeli military, with orders from Prime Minister Netanyahu, has orchestrated a "war against Hamas" and has been massacring the innocent ever since. As of this writing: forty-three thousand Palestinians dead, 70 percent being women and children, and over one hundred thousand wounded with the forced displacement of nearly two million Palestinians, more than 60 percent of their homes in Gaza destroyed. Israeli soldiers have bombed hospitals, refugee camps, schools, mosques, and UN centers and have murdered scores of journalists with the justification that Hamas must be eliminated. World leaders, humanitarian organizations, and the United Nations are calling for a cease-fire. Israel has responded with increased bombardment from air, sea, and land. They direct Palestinians to relocate to a different part of Gaza and then they bomb these "safe" zones. Israel has a stranglehold on basic supplies: food, water, medical, electricity, fuel, and communications. Through hunger and infectious disease, the indiscriminate bombardment's death toll will be surpassed by death from starvation and disease, if it hasn't already. Thousands of bodies remain buried under rubble from the bombing.

Israeli military are now bombing Lebanon. The death toll is in the thousands. The Biden administration's response? "Israel has a right to defend itself." The U.S. government is supplying them with weapons, doling out a $3.8 billion annual handout in military aid and promising billions more to support, fortify, and assist in this murderous campaign.

The U.S. has two warships standing by in the Middle East. Iran fired some one hundred eighty missiles into Israeli territory. Israel responded with U.S. military and political cover. Widening the war to other nations in the region is inevitable.

South Africa has brought charges against Israel, asserting it is committing genocide in Gaza. The International Court of Justice is currently hearing the case. They have documented five hundred statements that point to Israel's intention to commit genocide against the people of Palestine.

Lest we forget, Israel possesses nuclear weapons. This allows the Israeli government to slaughter with conventional weapons with impunity (as long as the nuclear red line is not crossed). The same thinking goes for U.S. and Russia. If you wear the nuclear crown and wave its scepter, the rest of the world are your subjects. These three nations are pushing the limits to see how much dominion the bomb gives them. It will allow the remaining nuclear nations to do likewise. The A-bomb incinerates (again) without being dropped.

I took part in a demonstration in Pennsylvania where two hundred people marched for a cease-fire. Jews, Christians, and Palestinians together crying out for an end to this genocide. A Hasidic rabbi, Dovid Feldman, spoke so eloquently about the Jewish faith as a religion of peace and cooperation. He pointed out, "Zionism is a political movement that has nothing to do with Judaism." He held a sign saying, "Judaism condemns the State of Israel and its atrocities."

He went on to say, "It was us Jewish people, it is our communities, it was our families, who suffered and were killed and tortured in the Holocaust. We know what suffering is! And we don't want to see this happen to anyone."

Dan, your message of nonviolence is needed now more than ever. God help us at the hands of men who only know the diplomacy of "Kill first. Then kill again."

Plowshares Actions

The hammer of the prophet Isaiah has continued to turn swords into plowshares. How could you have imagined that the first Plowshares action in 1980 you and Phil and others committed would inspire people to do the same forty-three years later. Calling themselves the Kings Bay Plowshares, Claire Grady, Martha Hennessy, Liz McAlister, Father Steve Kelly, Carmen Trotta, Mark Coville, and Patrick O'Neill entered Kings Bay Naval Submarine Base in Georgia on April 4, 2018. They acted on the prophet Isaiah's command to "beat swords into plowshares." They were superb in the courtroom, unveiling the Trident submarine as the most horrific weapons system in history—a doomsday machine, the tool of omnicide—and quoting Pope Francis's statement condemning the possession of nuclear weapons. Their jail sentences ranged from several months to your fellow Jesuit, Steve Kelly, serving just short of three years. Steve has transmitted the spirit of disarmament like no other. I believe he has surpassed your brother, Phil, in time spent in prison, well over ten years behind bars for a world without weapons.

Pray for Isaiah's vision that humanity may live in peace and for those who carry out this prophecy.

The Beatitudes

Father John Dear is the founder and executive director of The Beatitudes Center for the Nonviolent Jesus. On his website under the heading Staff is listed "Jesus of Nazareth, CEO." The purpose of this nonprofit organization is to teach and promote the nonviolence of Jesus, to help end violence, and to create a new culture of nonviolence through workshops, podcasts, and conferences. John is creating a presence online by inviting many high-profile activists to his podcast. His latest book, *The Gospel of Peace*, was published last spring.

Pray for John.

Your Confessor and Iconographer

Father Bill McNichols has painted your image as icon, to be remembered, inspired by, a vehicle for intercession in prayer. Since your departure, he has created a gallery of holy people, including Thomas Merton, whose lives are dedicated to peace and justice in one form or another. His new book with Christopher Pramuk, *All My Eyes See*, was released in the spring. He refers to you as a "blowtorch of honesty" and "a revolutionary against the war on children."

Little did I know that you asked Bill to be your confessor decades ago, priest to priest, friend to friend, humbling yourself before him, before God. I can only imagine the level of trust you possessed in Bill to share the Sacrament of Reconciliation.

Pray for Bill and Christopher.

Spirituality

I'm reading Sister Joan Chittister's *The Monastic Heart*. She writes that chant, as a contemplative practice,

> raises the mind and heart to God. It elevates consciousness beyond the prosaic and the earthly. It separates us from one kind of world and introduces us to another: the one that probes the soul rather than the mind. The one that settles us into the direction of our lives. The one that shapes our souls and trains the ears of our hearts to hear the spirit of life within us. The one that turns our feet from the path of the popular to the path of human purpose.

I remember you saying, "If the pope could be a woman, Joan Chittister would be the first." She inspires me and brings together action and contemplation in the spirit of Saint Benedict. The work for peace, justice, and social change guided by a contemplative mind and heart, minus the bear trap of ego.

Pray for Sister Joan.

I'm teaching a form of prayer that incorporates movement, breath, gesture, and chant followed by silence as entrance into contemplation. Less words, more God.

I really need your prayers now more than ever.

Berrigan Family

Updates on your family. Liz McAlister is in a beautiful facility living with dementia. Steve Kelly and I visited Liz with Frida and Kate. Father Steve celebrated Eucharist and Liz contributed to reflecting on the readings of the day with clarity, insight, and heartfulness. Her biblical mind remains intact. We shared a box of cookies from our favorite bakery, and she consumed with a similar enthusiasm to the Body of Christ. Multiple communions!

Afterwards, we had an outstanding epicurean feast with the entire gang in New London: Frida, Patrick, Seamus, Madeline (Rosena was not home at the time), Kate, and Karen (Kate's partner). They follow in the footsteps of the elder Berrigans: loving, caring, contributing, affirming all good in life. They breathe community. Patrick was the executive chef with various sous-chefs on hand. A feast that rivaled even your culinary efforts at the cottage with, of course, a "modest dessert."

Jerry and Molly continue living the Beatitudes in community at the Kalamazoo Peace House, ministering to the underprivileged and resisting death in all its masquerades. Jerry resembles Phil more each day, both in looks and speech. I have to do a double take at times.

Carol Berrigan, your sister-in-law, died after a long run with dementia. She apparently was pleasant and smiling during most of her illness.

Carla Berrigan has been a full-time caregiver for her husband, Marc, who has early-onset dementia. She has been a force behind this new edition of your poetry with Sue Hagedorn. Carla runs marathons like a kitchen faucet runs water, with no sign of running out! I haven't been in touch with the others in the Berrigan clan. Maybe you can report from your perch?

Pray for the Berrigans as I believe they have prayed to you.

I'll be on-island in the spring for a reading of the new release of *Block Island: Poems, Photos, and Letters.*

I miss your friendship, mentoring, cooking, stories, walks on the beach, island dinner parties, mailing your correspondence, keeping your cottage as tidy as a "captain's quarters," and Eucharist with you.

If you get time, drop a line, or save the postage and shoot me a dream.

—Jim

Afterword
by Carla Berrigan

My uncle Dan was the coolest and most exotic person I knew growing up. He'd show up from places around the world wearing one of his famous hats with a backpack swung over his shoulder carrying a few books, a toothbrush, a Ball canning jar filled with cherries soaked in whatever he had on hand to share with my father, and some relic or piece of art that he picked up on his travels to give to my parents who were the keepers of the family curio. My uncle Dan also had a little cottage on a bluff, out in the ocean, overlooking the sea!

This cottage was a special place. The place on the bluff. The opportunity to spend time here was anything but common. The cottage was offered to friends as a respite, a place to recharge. He shared the cottage with people who dedicated their lives to resistance. It was a place to pray, write, maybe refill the soul. It was a place snuggled in spectacular views no matter the season or the weather. If it had been suggested to Dan that he rent the place out, he would have brushed off the idea with the wave of his hand that he tended to do, always with a little flick to punctuate the gesture. I remember a little handwritten note in a frame placed on a bookcase in the bedroom referring to the cottage as "Exempt Acres." Where people needn't be wealthy to visit the beauty of the island (but if you wanted to buy a tank of propane or some fencing to keep the deer away from the new plantings, that would be okay). That was the extent of Dan's expectations.

My husband Marc and I were among the lucky ones. Dan generously scheduled time for us every year at the end of July before my parents arrived for the first two weeks in August. The timing, I'm sure, was for us to get the place sparkling and in primo condition before they arrived. It was at his cottage where I sat out on the deck one brilliant morning reading the original edition of *Block Island* for the first time. Dan had inscribed my copy with "Because you were there and will be!" The book felt alive to me. I could look up from the pages to the house where Bill Stringfellow and Anthony Towne lived, imagining the FBI lurking, posing as birdwatchers in a tropical storm, or over at the spot where Anthony Towne's ashes were buried amid unrelenting wind and pelting rain.

A dazzling dervish nor'easter, rain
striking like blue nails. Bill and I
two faulty frames, dug a small grave.
We lowered the box
no longer than a jeweler's casket shrining
a jeweled time piece. His heart stilled.

Looking over the bluffs out to the sea, sitting in that very setting that filled the pages of this beautiful little book moved me. The words were alive!

A porch facing the sea
September noon, late summer haze receding.
Like dazed microbe, over a microscope
I'm ferreting out Greek scripture,
word for word. Wonderful!

When Sue Hagedorn approached me with the idea of reprinting the book with Dan's letters and photographs, of course I was thrilled! My father had saved all correspondence between Dan, Phil, and himself and faithfully sent them off to DePaul University for decades. The letters became part of the Berrigan Archives. I was able to retrieve letters specifically written by Dan to my father and mother from or about Block Island with the help of Morgen MacIntosh Hodgetts, Coordinator of Special Collections and Archives.[1] Reading the letters filled with Dan's slang and creative spellings drew laughter and joy:

> The BI thing was cut short doo to 2 a series of teknikle catastrophes. It was coldern hell's walk in freezer + the furnace gave out. I was willing 2 be minor league heroic until 1 day. Sitten' in the sun + pickin' my nose, I heerd waters of Siloe under me. Examination revealed (you gessed) a spraying pipe. No plumber. Bill away for the day. fin'ley called Mr.Larson who responded, w-flashlight, pointed out turn off. I crawled in, did it, but the episode sorta broke the honeymoon.[2]

Collecting the letters and the photographs offered by friends brought the people whom I love and miss into the space around me as the memories came alive in my heart. It is my hope this new edition will bring the readers a deeper connection to the story told from the cottage on the bluff.

---

1. The Daniel Berrigan papers, Jerome C. Berrigan papers, and Philip Berrigan and Liz McAlister papers are available for research access in the Special Collections and Archives department in DePaul University's John T. Richardson Library in Chicago, Illinois.
2. Daniel Berrigan to Dears, December 9, 1980. Jerome C. Berrigan papers, box 5, folder 19. Special Collections and Archives, Depaul University Library, Chicago, IL.

Acknowledgments

Thanks to Willie Reale, Tom Reale and his supportive Brown Books staff, particularly Ben Davidoff and Brittany Griffiths.

Thanks as well to the Reale brothers' mom, Lyn, for her gorgeous picture of Dan, left on an unprocessed roll of film with her son, Willie.

About the Author

Daniel Berrigan (1921–2016) was a legendary priest, poet, peacemaker, author, teacher, and peace activist. He was the first priest in U.S. history ever arrested for nonviolent civil disobedience against war, and he is regarded as one of the greatest peacemakers of the twentieth century. He was nominated several times for the Nobel Peace Prize, won the Lamont Poetry award for his first collection of poetry, and was featured on the cover of TIME magazine. He was arrested over two hundred times in protest against war, injustice, and nuclear weapons; was a member of the 1968 Catonsville Nine antiwar action, for which he spent several years in prison; and the 1980 Plowshares Eight anti-nuclear action, for which he faced ten years in prison.

Daniel Berrigan was the author of over fifty books of poetry, journals, plays, essays, theology, and scripture studies, such as *No Bars to Manhood*; *The Dark Night of Resistance*; *Time Without Number*; *We Die Before We Live*; *False Gods, Real Men*; *America Is Hard to Find*; *Isaiah; Wisdom*; *Jeremiah*; *Job*; *Testimony*; and his autobiography *To Dwell in Peace*. His play, *The Trial of the Catonsville Nine*, continues to be performed around the world. *Daniel*

Berrigan: Essential Writings as well as *And the Risen Bread: Collected Poems* were edited by John Dear.

Daniel Berrigan also served as a hospital chaplain, and he taught at Yale, Fordham, Georgetown, the Graduate Theology Union, Berea College, and elsewhere. For further information, visit: www.DanielBerrigan.org and www.BerriganCollective.org.

About the Editors

Susan Hagedorn

Susan Hagedorn earned a BA in English at Ohio Wesleyan University, a BS in nursing at the University of Massachusetts, an MS in maternal-child nursing at Boston College, an MA in Media Studies at The New School, and a PhD in nursing at the University of Colorado, where she taught, practiced as a nurse practitioner, and did research. Sue's nursing career has been dedicated to social justice as a nurse educator, nurse practitioner, philanthropist, filmmaker, and activist.

Sue "retired" from nursing academia to a career in documentary filmmaking. She has produced more than fifteen films focused on nursing and social justice, including films advocating for a variety of roles within the practice of nursing and celebrating nursing history. She also made a feature about a hate crime on Long Island (*Deputized,* 2013), followed by two Berrigan films: *Seeking Shelter: A Story of Place, Faith, and Resistance* (2018) and *The Berrigans: Devout and Dangerous* (2021) about the Berrigans' century of peacemaking.

Susan is the recipient of the Thomas Jefferson Award, the Florence Nightingale Award for Excellence in Health and Care Analytics, and the Humanitarian Award, which she received for *Deputized* at the Long Island

International Film Expo. She is also a fellow of the American Academy of Nursing and the American Association of Nurse Practitioners. She lives part-time on Block Island and is co-president of the Block Island Historical Society.

Carla Berrigan

Carla Berrigan, beloved niece of Daniel, spent thirty-seven years being a literacy advocate to inner-city children in Syracuse, New York. Her annual respite in Dan's cottage on Block Island nourished and replenished her spirit to continue her vocation as an educator and proliferator of the peace and justice work that is the legacy of her family.

Since Carla's retirement from the Syracuse City School District in 2023, her main focus has been caring for her cherished husband, Marc, who courageously battled the final stages of a rare form of early-onset dementia. Carla's practice of long-distance running keeps her strong for this work.